A GREAT SEA MYSTERY

By the same Author :

MYSTERIES OF THE SEA
PERIL OF THE SEA
STRANGE ADVENTURES OF THE SEA
HERE ARE MYSTERIES

THE MARY CELESTE.   DECEMBER 5TH, 1872.

A GREAT
SEA MYSTERY

The true story of
THE "MARY CELESTE"

By
J. G. LOCKHART

First Edition 1927

CONTENTS

CHAPTER		PAGE
	INTRODUCTION	9
I	THE FINDING OF THE SHIP	15
II	THE *Mary Celeste*	31
III	AT GIBRALTAR	38
IV	SOME THEORIES	52
V	THE STORY OF HABAKUK JEPHSON	61
VI	" SOLUTIONS "	74
VII	MORE SOLUTIONS	80
VIII	THE STORY OF ABEL FOSDYK	84
IX	THE STORY OF TRIGGS	97
X	THE STORY OF JOHN PEMBERTON	108
XI	THE TRUTH	121
XII	THE SEQUEL	135

INTRODUCTION

No story of the sea has ever perplexed and fascinated men so strangely as the affair of the *Mary Celeste*. There is something about that conundrum of an empty ship, found in mid-ocean, with not a soul aboard and not a clue to explain what mischance had befallen her, which has never failed to draw to itself alike lovers of the sea and lovers of mysteries. During the fifty-five years which have passed since the men of the *Dei Gratia* sighted the famous derelict, a voluminous literature has gathered round the story, most of it, let it be confessed, not of a very high order, and much of it inspired rather by a craving for the sensational than by a regard for historical accuracy ; as though the unembellished tale were not enough. But this literature, garbled or otherwise, is at least a witness to the abiding interest of the problem, and is itself

A GREAT SEA MYSTERY

my justification for trying to do in these pages what has never yet been done : to set out in full the plain facts that we know, to weigh the evidence as impartially as is possible, to test the different theories that from time to time have been put forward, and, by the light of our information, to reach a conclusion.

There is an additional reason for making an attempt of this kind to sum up the whole story. The *Mary Celeste* presents an irresistible temptation to the romancer. Scarcely a year goes by without the appearance of some new " solution," announced with headlines and received with congratulation, disposing, more or less ingeniously, of the mystery from the record of a long-concealed survivor or a lately discovered document. Some of these " solutions," regarded simply as fiction, make excellent reading ; but every one that I have examined is a plain and demonstrable invention.

These literary enterprises, apart from any question of morality, have had one unfor-

INTRODUCTION

tunate result; they have surrounded the story with a cloud of imaginary circumstances which obscure the truth and make it by no means an easy task to extract fact from fancy.

It may be said that this does not greatly matter, for, after all, the *Mary Celeste* and her fate are not of sufficient historical importance to warrant too meticulous a regard for accuracy. Yet it must be remembered that relatives of some who sailed in her and in her salvor, the *Dei Gratia*, are alive to-day in the United States, and that it is scarcely pleasant for them to read " solutions " which for their authors' purposes lightheartedly convey the gravest charges against Captain Briggs or Captain Morehouse or other members of the ships' companies. These unfortunate relatives have no remedy in law, for neither in Great Britain nor in the United States is there redress for a libel upon the dead; but their grievance is none the less real, and their feelings should be all the more considered.

A GREAT SEA MYSTERY

Let me give another example of the work of the romancers. In a book [1] which I wrote nearly three years ago, I gave what I believed to be a full and accurate account of the story so far as I was able to do so from the information then available to me. I even suggested a solution which I felt might cover the facts without laying too much strain upon the credulity of my readers. I wrote in all good faith. The book was published ; it brought me letters from numbers of people in different parts of the world ; and in course of time I received a great deal of fresh and authentic material from the United States, Gibraltar and elsewhere, which, pieced together, put a very different complexion on the whole affair. I found that in one or two important particulars I had been misled ; that I had reported as a fact at least one incident which came straight from the brain of a romancer ; and that the problem admitted of a plainer explanation than I had supposed.

[1] *Mysteries of the Sea.*

INTRODUCTION

These are, in the main, my reasons for returning to a subject on which so much has been written, and for endeavouring, once and for all time, to tell the story of the finding of the *Mary Celeste*, three hundred miles from Gibraltar, on the afternoon of December 5th, 1872, and of the fate of her crew.

I cannot end this introduction without expressing my indebtedness to Mr. Frederick Shepard, Dr. Oliver Cobb, Mr. R. L. Sprague, Miss Daly, and many others, without whose assistance this book could never have been written.

A GREAT SEA MYSTERY

CHAPTER I

THE FINDING OF THE SHIP

AT three o'clock, or thereabouts, in the afternoon of December 5th,[1] 1872, the *Dei Gratia*, a brig of Nova Scotia, bound from New York to Gibraltar under the command of Captain Morehouse, was about one hundred and thirty miles from the coast of Portugal. To be exact, she was in latitude 37.17 N., longitude 18.20 W. In some accounts slightly different bearings have been given, but the above, which are taken from the American Maritime Register, are probably correct. At any rate, the *Dei*

---

[1] Many accounts give December 4th as the date ; December 5th, however, is the day given in the report of the Attorney-General for Gibraltar to the Board of Trade.

A GREAT SEA MYSTERY

Gratia had covered about two-thirds of the distance from the Azores to the Straits of Gibraltar, on a course a little to the north of the direct route.

The sea was calm and there was a light wind from the north. There were, it is said, two other vessels within sight of the *Dei Gratia*. The first of these was a German tramp steamer outward bound for the West Indies. Later, when she reached port and heard talk of a derelict found under rather queer circumstances, the tramp's crew asserted that they remembered sighting, on the day and in the latitude mentioned, a strange brig about three miles to starboard. They had signalled to her, and had been a little puzzled when no reply was forthcoming. It had argued a want of sea manners, but the distance between the two ships was too great, and the matter was too trivial, to engage further attention.

It must have been a little later on in the afternoon that the *Dei Gratia*, sailing on the port tack, began to overhaul this same

FINDING OF THE SHIP

strange brig, which had all her sails set and was on the port tack, her headsails, however (jib and foretopmast staysail), being set to starboard. As the *Dei Gratia* came up with her, Captain Morehouse, rather to his surprise, recognised her as the *Mary Celeste*, which had been loading her cargo in New York at the same time as the *Dei Gratia*, but which had put to sea a few days earlier. He and Briggs, the Master of the *Mary Celeste*, were old acquaintances, and had actually dined together in New York on the night before the *Mary Celeste* sailed.[1] It was therefore only natural that Captain Morehouse, by way of passing the time of day with his friend, should have signalled to the other ship. It was not so natural that the *Mary Celeste* should keep on, as she did, without vouchsafing any reply. And, as the interval between the two ships diminished, Captain Morehouse was still more puzzled by the haphazard sailing of the *Mary Celeste ;* for instead of making a steady

[1] On the authority of Mrs. Morehouse, the Captain's wife.

A GREAT SEA MYSTERY

course, she was yawing and, when the wind shifted a point, she would run off aimlessly before it. Yet another circumstance struck him as strange : whereas both ships were sailing on the port tack, the jib and foretopmast staysail of the *Mary Celeste* were set on the starboard tack. Obviously, there was something amiss aboard her, and when Captain Morehouse called to his mate to have a look at the other ship, and asked him what he thought was the matter, the mate at once made the obvious answer that it looked as though the crew were below drunk.

By this time the two ships were about half a mile from each other. Still no answer came from the *Mary Celeste*, nor, scan her decks as they might, could the men in the *Dei Gratia* detect a sign of life aboard. They gave her an urgent hoist and, a few moments later, as the two ships drove yet closer to each other, Captain Morehouse hailed the brig. When, in despite of every signal, her decks remained silent and empty, he began to feel seriously alarmed, and

FINDING OF THE SHIP

ordered a boat to be lowered and manned by the second mate, Oliver Deveau (or Devon) and a couple of men.

The boat was soon under way, and as it neared the brig the three men could see the name, plainly painted upon her stern—*Mary Celeste, New York*. That was the end of any doubts they might have had of her identity. So far as they could see, as they came alongside, there was nothing wrong with her. Here was no water-logged derelict, but a well-found craft, her sails set, her timbers undamaged, and yet apparently not a soul aboard her. What was the explanation—mutiny, or piracy, or something worse ?

Coming alongside, the mate ordered one of the men to stay in the boat, while he and the other clambered up by the chain plates and hoisted themselves aboard. On deck there was not a soul to be seen, or a sound to be heard but the thud of their footsteps, the creaking of the blocks, and the occasional slap of a sail. There was no one at the wheel;

A GREAT SEA MYSTERY

the brig, it seemed, was sailing herself, unless, like the Phantom Ship of the old story, she was manned by a supernatural crew. Completely mystified, and possibly a little alarmed, the mate signalled to Captain Morehouse to join him.

With the arrival of the Master of the *Dei Gratia*, a careful examination of the ship began. Cautiously the two men walked aft, looking keenly about them ; then forward again ; and then below deck. They searched the ship from stem to stern, and neither in cabin, nor in forecastle, nor in hold was a man to be seen, or any visible sign of trouble to be detected. They came at last to a standstill, as baffled a pair of men as were to be found on the high seas. Here was a ship undoubtedly derelict, and yet, so far as they could observe, perfectly sound. Her hull, masts and yards were in good condition ; her cargo, which apparently consisted of a number of barrels of alcohol, was properly stowed and in apple-pie order ; and there was no lack of food or water. On deck, it is

FINDING OF THE SHIP

true, one small point drew their attention. One of the hatches over the hold had been displaced and lay, wrong side up, close to the hatchway it had covered. That was not much of a clue on which to fasten.

What was almost as puzzling as the absence of any living person aboard was the lack of a trace, not only of a reason for evacuating the ship, but of the actual process of evacuation. One would at least have expected to find marks of disorder or of confusion ; but there was nothing. It was as though the men of the *Mary Celeste* had been pursuing their usual routine when, by some strange agency, they had been spirited away.

In the forecastle, for example, the seamen's chests were untouched ; some razors which were lying about were bright and unrusted, and garments were hanging out to dry on a line ; while among the dunnage were an English note for five pounds and other articles which, though of no great value, were, one might have supposed, suffi-

A GREAT SEA MYSTERY

ciently precious to be taken by their owners when the ship was abandoned.

In the galley everything was in good order, just as the cook would have left it after he had cleared away the aftermath of a meal.

The cabin, again, yielded very little in the way of a clue. There was a melodeon or harmonium. Its cover was raised as though it had been in recent use, and on a rack near by was an open sheet of music ; on the table there was a sewing-machine with a piece of cloth that might have been a child's pinafore fixed in it, and a small oil can, a thimble, and a reel of cotton, all of them objects easily displaced by the motion of the ship, lay on the table beside it. On the same table there was a slate containing some notes for the log, and showing November 25th as the date for the last entry ; and there was an unfinished letter, apparently from the mate of the *Mary Celeste* to his wife, beginning, " Fanny, my dear wife." The writer had got so far when something had happened to interrupt him. There were books and music, mostly of a

FINDING OF THE SHIP

religious character, undisturbed and un-
harmed, and spare panes of glass were found
stowed away and unbroken. The Captain's
watch was hanging from the lamp bracket
over the table. According to some accounts,
the accuracy of which I would not care to
guarantee, there were also the remains of a
half-eaten breakfast in the cabin, a plate
with a little porridge in it, and an egg with
the top sliced off. The general inference
drawn from an inspection of the cabin was
that, whatever might have been the nature of
the mysterious calamity which had turned
the *Mary Celeste* into a derelict, it was not
stress of weather.

In the Captain's cabin some further curious discoveries were made. Trinkets of
some small value, and including at least one
gold locket, had been left behind, and in
one of the bunks which looked as though it
had been occupied by a child, the imprint
of a head was still clearly visible on a pillow.
As the other berths in the cabin had all been
made up, it seemed reasonable to conclude

A GREAT SEA MYSTERY

that the ship must have been abandoned in the late morning or afternoon, a conclusion which perhaps goes rather against the story of the breakfast *débris*.

Clearly there had been a great hurry, and the crew had had time to take very little with them. One of the drawers in the store-room had the appearance of having been hastily emptied of some tins of preserved meat; the ship's papers, with the exception of the log-book, were missing; and there was no sign of the Captain's chronometer.

This was all very puzzling; and when we come to the further and slightly sinister discoveries made by the men from the *Dei Gratia*, we are no nearer to a solution. The first of these discoveries was a cutlass which they found, and which, when taken out of its scabbard, showed signs of having been smeared with blood and afterwards wiped. The idea of foul play, which this at once suggested, was supported by the detection of what looked like spots of blood on the deck, close to the displaced hatch which has

FINDING OF THE SHIP

been mentioned a little earlier. Yet more stains, which might have been blood, were also observed on the starboard topgallant rail, and close to them a deep cut, such as a sharp axe might have made, was detected. We shall hear more of these marks later.

The other discovery, which was to give rise to a great deal of speculation, seemed quite without meaning. On either side of the bows of the ship, some two or three feet above the water-line, a narrow strip had been cut away from the edge of one of the outer planks, to a depth of about three-eighths of an inch, a width of about an inch and a-quarter, and a length of about between six and seven feet. The injury was recent, obviously intentional, and apparently caused by some sharp cutting instrument.

The search of the ship having yielded so little to explain her abandonment, Captain Morehouse next turned to the log. The last day's work recorded was on November 24th, eleven days earlier, when an observation taken placed the vessel in latitude 36° 56′ N.

25

THE AZORES

SAN MIGUEL

FORMIGAS

SANTA MARIA

MILES
0 10 20 30 40

Ax represents the position of the 'MARY CELESTE' at noon on Nov. 24th.
The dotted line represents her approximate course between noon on Nov. 24th. and 8 a.m. on Nov. 25th.
Bx represents her position at 8 a.m on Nov 25th.

FINDING OF THE SHIP

and longitude 27° 20' W. ; in other words about one hundred and ten miles due west of the island of Santa Maria in the Azores. Entries on the slate, however, had been carried on up to 8 a.m. on the following morning, when apparently the ship was passing north of the island, the eastern point of which, at the time of the entry, bore S.S.W. at a distance of six miles. That was the last record of any kind, and the problem, as it appeared at once to Captain Morehouse, and as it remains for us to-day, is what could have happened after eight o'clock on the morning of November 25th, and how the *Mary Celeste*, unmanned and unsteered, held on her course for the better part of ten days and nights, until she reached the point, some seven hundred and fifty miles east of the island of Santa Maria, where the *Dei Gratia* found her.

Her sailing, of course, is not so improbable as it sounds. I have mentioned that when Captain Morehouse sighted the *Mary Celeste* he was puzzled to observe that, while she

27

A GREAT SEA MYSTERY

was sailing on the port tack, her jib and foretopmast staysail were set on the starboard tack. Dr. Oliver Cobb, to whom I shall have occasion to refer later, suggests a perfectly feasible explanation. He assumes that just before her abandonment the *Mary Celeste* was sailing east with a southerly wind. Something—whatever it may have been—happened. The yards were at once swung round to lay the square sails back, and the ship was hove-to on the starboard tack, a natural preliminary to getting a boat away. Later, when the vessel had been deserted by its crew, the wind changed to north, and the brig sailed off on an easterly course, with her square sails full and her main boom swinging over. With her sails set as they were, and the wind blowing steadily from the north, when she came to the wind the head-sails would back her off ; when she fell away the mainsail would drive her into the wind again. Her natural course would therefore be roughly at a right angle to the direction of the wind, and might well

FINDING OF THE SHIP

take her to the spot where she met the *Dei Gratia*.

Even so, to cover a distance of seven hundred and fifty miles, in ten days and in the right direction, was pretty good going for an unmanned ship, and it is doubtful whether a craft or any other rig, except possibly a barquentine, could have managed it.

With these unsatisfying results, the search for the moment ended. Captain Morehouse could make nothing of the business ; but, whatever the explanation might be, salvage was salvage, and a windfall that does not drop on every day of the week. So the mate and two men being left aboard to work the derelict, the two ships continued their interrupted voyage to Gibraltar.

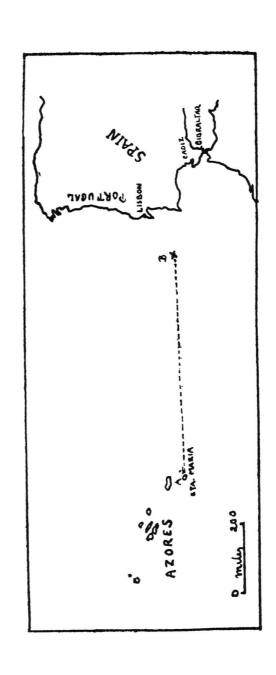

CHAPTER II

THE *Mary Celeste*

A FEW years ago someone wrote a letter to the *Nautical Magazine* [1] in which he stated that he had made inquiries about the *Mary Celeste* at Lloyd's, and had been " laughed out of court." The story, he was assured, had been carefully examined and found to be a myth. The gentleman's inquiries cannot have been very exhaustive, and his informant can scarcely have been anyone of experience at Lloyd's, as not only are the main facts, as I have just related them, established beyond dispute, but in no less than six separate numbers of *Lloyd's List* in 1872 and 1873 are the *Mary Celeste* and her misadventure mentioned.[2] The first

[1] July, 1922.

[2] December 16th, December 17th, 1872. March 1st, March 18th, March 25th, September 17th, 1873.

31

A GREAT SEA MYSTERY

entry reports her arrival at Gibraltar with three men from the *Dei Gratia* aboard, the second the taking over of the ship by the Admiralty Court, and the third her departure for Genoa. The other three entries record her movements after leaving Gibraltar. As *Lloyd's List* is most emphatically an organ of fact and not of legend, we may take the existence and salving of the *Mary Celeste* as proved.

In the American Record of Shipping she appears as a half-brig or brigantine of 282 tons, built in 1861 at Parrsborough in Nova Scotia. Her tonnage has been variously given as 206 and 236, not to mention many other figures extravagantly wide of the mark ; the point is not very important, but 282 is probably correct. She was, therefore, a two-masted ship with square sails on her foremast and fore and aft sails on her mainmast. Her length was 98 feet, her beam 25 feet, and her draught 11 feet 2 inches. She was christened the *Amazon*, but her name was soon changed to the *Mary Sellers*,

THE *MARY CELESTE*

which, in course of years and maltreatment by many tongues, was corrupted into *Mary Celeste*, an odd hybrid of Latin and Saxon.

In 1872 her principal owner was Captain James H. Winchester, of the firm of J. H. Winchester & Company, New York, but three other men,[1] one of whom was Captain Briggs, held shares in the ship, and a certain Mr. Hart had a mortgage on it.

We learn from the Maritime Register that the *Mary Celeste* (often misnamed the *Marie Celeste*) sailed from New York for Genoa on November 7th, 1872, under the command of Captain Benjamin S. Briggs, of Marion, Massachusetts. As some of the so-called explanations of the mystery which have appeared in print show Captain Briggs in what, to put it mildly, can only be described as a most unfavourable light, I am anxious to make it clear that, from all evidence obtainable, he bore the highest character, both at his home in New England, where he and his

[1] Daniel T. Sanson, 2/24 ; Sylvester Goodwin, 2/24; Benjamin S. Briggs, 8/24.

A GREAT SEA MYSTERY

family were well-known and much respected, and also in Gibraltar, where his frequent calls had made him a familiar figure. He was a man of about forty-five, ruddy of complexion and whiskered, and has been described by those who knew him best as a typical sailing-master of what is termed the old school ; that is, he was a bit of a disciplinarian, a strict teetotaller, and, weather permitting, made it his daily practice when at sea to read a chapter of the Bible.

When he sailed on his last voyage he left behind him in New Bedford his grandmother Mrs. Nathan Briggs, his son Arthur, aged seven, and his cousin Oliver Cobb, then a boy of fourteen, who had been living with him, and to whom I am indebted for much of this information about the family. I mention these details because they hardly represent the family circumstances of a bully, or a swindler, or a homicidal maniac, all of which pleasing rôles have been assigned by various charitable chroniclers to Captain Briggs ; and because these gentlemen, in

THE *MARY CELESTE*

their zeal to provide a solution to the mystery of the *Mary Celeste*, have quite omitted to consider the distress which their ill-founded speculations must cause to the relatives and friends of the men who disappeared.

Captain Briggs was accompanied by his wife Sarah, who had sailed with him on previous voyages, and by their little daughter, aged two, from whom, as she was little more than a baby, her mother did not wish to be separated.

Before I quit the subject of the Briggs family, I ought to mention a tragic coincidence which befell them about this time, and which has been recorded by Dr. Cobb. Captain Briggs had a brother Oliver, also a master-mariner, who, a short while before the *Mary Celeste* left New York, had himself sailed in the brig *Julia A. Hallock*, bound for Vigo, and later for some port in the Mediterranean. The two brothers in correspondence had tentatively arranged to meet in the spring of 1873 at Barcelona, where they were to load fruit for the homeward

A GREAT SEA MYSTERY

voyage to New York. When two days out from Vigo, however, the *Julia A. Hallock* ran into heavy weather in the Bay of Biscay and sprang a leak. She was carrying a cargo of fine coal, which choked the pumps so badly that they became unworkable. The ship filled with water, turned over and sank, all on board perishing except the second mate, Perry, who, after drifting about for four days on a piece of wreckage, was picked up by a Spanish vessel. This disaster, in which Captain Oliver Briggs lost his life, must have preceded by only a short time the tragedy which overtook the *Mary Celeste* and her master, Captain Benjamin Briggs ; and it may be remarked that, had it not been for the fortunate rescue of Perry, we should know no more of the fate of the *Julia A. Hallock* than we know of that of the *Mary Celeste*.

In addition to Captain Briggs and his wife and child, the *Mary Celeste* carried a crew of seven men. The first mate was Albert G. Richardson, of Maine, the second mate was Andrew Gilling, of New York, the

36

THE *MARY CELESTE*

steward and cook was Edward William Head, of New York ; the rest of the company were Germans, or of German origin, and their names were Volkerk Lorenzen, Bos Lorenzen, Arian Harbens and Gottlieb Goodshaad.[1]

There were, in all, therefore, ten people on board. In most of the numerous narratives of the *Mary Celeste* which have appeared, the authors have allowed themselves ample licence both as to the names and the number of the crew. The favourite number, as might be supposed, is thirteen, but the names vary widely and picturesquely.

The *Mary Celeste* carried a cargo of 1,700 barrels of alcohol, consigned to Messrs. H. Mascarenhas & Company of Genoa, and to be used for fortifying Italian wines.

[1] In no two accounts of the *Mary Celeste*, official and semi-official reports not excepted, are. the names of these men, where given correctly, spelt in the same way. The point being quite unimportant, I have followed my own fancy.

CHAPTER III

AT GIBRALTAR

THE arrival of the *Dei Gratia* with a derelict as consort and a strange story to tell created a considerable stir at Gibraltar. Apart from the interest which a maritime community would naturally take in so curious an event, the Captain of the *Mary Celeste*, as will be recalled, was well-known to and much respected by local residents. What, they asked at once, could have happened to him and his crew ? The men of the *Dei Gratia*, of course, were unable to answer this question ; they could only relate the facts, as they knew them, and having done so put in a claim for salvage. But before any award could be made, an inquiry had to be held, and the result of this inquiry was reported to the British Board of Trade by Mr. Solly Flood, " Her Majesty's

AT GIBRALTAR

Advocate-General and Proctor for the Queen in her Office of Admiralty, and Attorney-General for Gibraltar."

In view of all the conflicting versions which from time to time have appeared in print, I make no apology for giving, even at the cost of some repetition, Mr. Flood's report *verbatim*. It was official ; it was made at the time and on the spot ; and it was the result of a semi-judicial examination of the derelict and of her discoverers. As evidence, therefore, it is the most important document to which we can refer.

" I have the honour to acquaint you, for the information of the Privy Council for Trade, that early on the morning of December 13, part of the crew of the British vessel *Dei Gratia*, bound from New York for Gibraltar for orders, brought into this port a brigantine, which they stated they had found on the 5th of that month, in lat. 38.20 N., long. 17.15 W.[1]

[1] These bearings do not quite tally with those obtained from other sources, such as the American Maritime Register. See page 15

A GREAT SEA MYSTERY

at 3 p.m. sea time, totally abandoned and derelict, and which they supposed from the log to be the American brigantine *Mary Celeste*, bound from New York for Genoa. They stated that the wind being from the north, and the *Dei Gratia*, consequently, on the port tack, they met the derelict with her jib and foremast staysail set on the starboard tack. I caused the derelict to be arrested in the customary manner upon her arrival, whereupon the Master of the *Dei Gratia*, who had arrived on the evening of December 12th, made his claim for salvage. The second mate of the *Dei Gratia*, and those of her crew who had boarded the derelict, were examined in support of the claim to salvage on the 20th and 21st ult. But the account which they gave of the soundness and good condition of the derelict was so extraordinary that I found it necessary to apply for a survey, which was held in my presence on the 23rd of the same month, and the result of which is embodied in the affidavit

AT GIBRALTAR

of Mr. Ricardo Portunato, a diver, sworn on the 7th inst., of Mr. John Austin, Master Surveyor of Shipping, sworn on the 8th inst., and Mr. T. J. Vecchio, sworn on the 9th inst. From that survey it appears that both bows of the derelict had been recently cut by a sharp instrument, but that she was thoroughly sound, staunch, strong, and in every way seaworthy and well found ; that she was well provisioned, and that she had encountered no seriously heavy weather ; and that no appearance of fire or of explosion, or of alarm of fire or explosion, or any other assignable cause for abandonment, was discoverable. A sword, however, was found, which appeared to me to exhibit traces of blood, and to have been wiped before being returned into its scabbard. My opinion in this respect having been corroborated by others, I proceeded on the 7th inst., to make, with the assistance of the Marshal of the Vice-Admiralty Court, a still more minute examination for marks of violence,

A GREAT SEA MYSTERY

and I had the honour of being accompanied and greatly assisted by Captain Fitzroy, R.N., H.M.S. *Minotaur ;* Capt. Adeane, R.N., H.M.S. *Agincourt ;* Captain Dowell, C.B., R.N., H.M.S. *Hercules ;* Captain Vansittart, R.N., H.M.S. *Sultan ;* and by Colonel Laffan, R.E., all of whom agreed with me in opinion that the injury to the bows had been effected intentionally by a sharp instrument. On examining the starboard topgallant-rail, marks were discovered, apparently of blood, and a mark of a blow, apparently of a sharp axe. On descending through the fore hatch, a barrel, ostensibly of alcohol, appeared to have been tampered with. The vessel's Register, Manifest and Bills of Lading have not been found, neither has any sextant or chronometer been found. On the other hand, almost the whole personal effects of the Master, and, as I believe, of his wife and child, and of the crew, have been found in good order and condition. They are of considerable

AT GIBRALTAR

value. In the Captain's cabin were a harmonium in a rosewood case, books of music, and others mostly of a religious tendency ; gold lockets and other trinkets, jewellery, and female attire of a superior description, were in the lady's boxes. The working chart and ship's log were also found on the arrest of the vessel. Both are complete up to noon of the 24th November. I transmit a copy of the last day's work ; the deck or slate log is continued—copy of which is enclosed— up to 8 a.m. on the following day, at which hour the eastern point of St. Mary's (Azores) bore S.S.W., distant six miles. She had therefore run considerably less number of knots since the previous noon than that entered in the slate, the longi- tude of St. Mary's being 25.9 W. Since then eight weeks have elapsed, and nothing whatever has been heard of the Master or crew, or of the unhappy lady and child. The ship's log, which was found on board, shows the last day's work

A GREAT SEA MYSTERY

of the ship up to noon on the 24th November, when the weather was sufficiently fine to enable an observation to be taken ; the position then was by observation lat. 36.56 N., long. 27.20 E. Entries on the log slate are carried up to 8 a.m. on the 25th, which is the last, and at which time she had passed from west to east to the north of the Island of St. Mary's, the eastern point of which bore S.S.W. six miles distant. The distance of the longitude of the place where she was found from that last mentioned on the log is 1.18 N., so that she must actually have held her course for ten days after November 25th, the wheel being loose all the time. My object is to move the Board of Trade to take such action as they may think fit to discover, if possible, the fate of the Master, his wife and child, and the crew of the derelict. My own theory or guess is, that the crew got at the alcohol, and in the fury of drunkenness murdered the Master, whose name was Briggs, his wife

AT GIBRALTAR

and child, and the chief mate ; that they
then damaged the bows of the vessel, with
the view of giving it the appearance of
having struck on rocks, or suffered a
collision, so as to induce the Master of any
vessel which might pick them up, if they
saw her at some distance, to think her not
worth attempting to save ; and that they
did, some time between the 25th November and the 5th December, escape on
board some vessel bound for some North
or South American port or the West
Indies."

In amplification of Mr. Flood's report we
have the affidavits of other qualified witnesses. The first is that of Mr. John Austin,
whose evidence was summarised in the
Shipping Gazette of February 5th.

"The affidavit of Mr. John Austin,
Surveyor of Shipping at Gibraltar, is of
considerable length, and he states that
the whole appearance of the vessel showed
that she had never encountered any such
violence as would have accounted for her

A GREAT SEA MYSTERY

abandonment. He found no wines or spirits on board. He made the most careful and minute examination through every part of the vessel to which he had access, and did not discover the slightest trace of there having been any explosion or any fire, or of anything calculated to create an alarm of an explosion or of fire. The vessel was thoroughly sound, staunch and strong, and not making water to any appreciable extent. He found on the bow, between two and three feet above the water line, on the port side, a long narrow strip of the edge of one of her outer planks cut away to the depths of about three-eights of an inch, and about one inch and a quarter wide, for length of about six or seven feet. The injury had been sustained very recently, and could not have been effected by weather, and was apparently done by a sharp cutting instrument continuously through the whole length of the injury. He found on the starboard bow, but a little further from the stem of

AT GIBRALTAR

the vessel, a precisely similar injury, but perhaps an eighth or a tenth of an inch wider, which in his opinion had been effected at the same time and by the same means. He adds that he was wholly unable to discover any reason whatever why the vessel was abandoned."

In the same number of the *Shipping Gazette* we find a *précis* of the evidence of Portunato, the diver.

" J. Ricardo Portunato the diver, who had examined the hull of the vessel, states in his affidavit that the vessel did not exhibit any trace of damage or injury, or any other appearance that the vessel had been in collision or had struck upon any rock or shoal or had met with any other accident or casualty. The hull, keel, sternpost and rudder were in thoroughly good order and condition."

To complete the contemporary evidence, I add the report of Captain Shufeldt, of the American ship *Plymouth*, an independent witness whose conclusions were published

47

A GREAT SEA MYSTERY

in the *Gibraltar Chronicle* of January 4th, 1873.

"We have been favoured with a copy of a report made by Captain Shufeldt, United States ship *Plymouth*, after a visit paid by him to the derelict *Mary Celeste*. Captain Shufeldt, with everyone who has examined the ship, is of opinion that she was abandoned by the master and crew without sufficient reason, probably in a moment of panic. He considers that she may have been strained in a gale and for the time leaked so much as seriously to alarm the master, and it is possible that at this time another vessel in sight induced him, as his wife and child were on board, to abandon his ship thus hastily. Should this surmise be correct the time which must elapse before he and his crew are again heard of must depend on the distance of the port to which the rescuing vessel happened to be bound. Captain Shufeldt altogether rejects the idea of a mutiny, because there is no evidence of

AT GIBRALTAR

violence about the decks or in the cabins, and, with regard to the damage about the bows of the ship, he considers that it amounts merely to splinters in the bending of the planks, which were afterwards forced off by the action of the sea, and not in any way betokening any intention of wilfully damaging the vessel. The *Mary Celeste* is confessed on all hands to be at the present moment staunch and seaworthy, and Captain Shufeldt maintains that the master and crew will either be heard of some day or, if not, that they have perished in the boat for which they abandoned their own ship. For the present the mystery remains unsolved, but it is satisfactory to note that the opinion of a practical man such as Captain Shufeldt, and an analysis made by Dr. Patron, of this city, of the alleged bloodstains, coincide in refuting the theory of violence. The possible fate of those who were on board the *Mary Celeste* is sad enough without the addition of mutiny and blood-

A GREAT SEA MYSTERY

shed. It will be observed that the opinion of Captain Shufeldt with regard to the marks on the ship's bows is in direct contradiction to that expressed by the surveyors here."

It is worth noting that in Mr. Flood's report there is one omission of some importance, particularly in view of the theory which he put forward. He makes no reference to the fact, which we learn from Captain Shufeldt and other sources, that on analysis the stains on the cutlass were found to be rust and not blood. On the other hand, he does allude to the apparently trivial discovery, which some of the witnesses who examined the ship's cargo omit to mention, that one of the barrels of alcohol in the hold had been started.

So we come to the verdict of the Vice-Admiralty Court, given on March 25th, as reported in the *Gibraltar Chronicle* of the following day.

" In the Vice-Admiralty Court yesterday the Hon. the Chief Justice gave judg-

AT GIBRALTAR

ment in the *Mary Celeste* salvage case, and awarded the sum of £1,700 to the master and crew of the Nova Scotia brigantine *Dei Gratia* for the salvage services rendered by them ; the costs of the suit to be paid out of the property salved. The *Mary Celeste* was valued at $5,700, and her cargo at $36,943, total $42,643, so that the award may be set down as one-fifth of the total value."

The judgment ended on a curious note of censure. It appears that Captain Morehouse had allowed his first mate, Oliver Deveau (or Devon) to obliterate some of the supposed stains of blood on the cutlass or the starboard topgallant rail. As a result, the rather expensive analysis of the remaining stains had been necessitated, and the cost of this was ordered by the judge to be charged against the amount which the salvors had been awarded.

CHAPTER IV

SOME THEORIES

IT will be observed that among those who were personally concerned with the enquiry and the examination of the *Mary Celeste* at Gibraltar opinions were sharply divided over the solution to the mystery. The most popular view was that of Mr. Solly Flood, who believed that the crew of the ship had got at the alcohol in the hold, murdered the Captain, his wife and child, and perhaps the chief mate, and then escaped to another vessel. That this was also the opinion of the Treasury Department at Washington appears from the instructions it issued to Customs officers.

" You are requested to furnish this Department with any information you may be able to obtain affording a clue which may lead to the discovery of all the

SOME THEORIES

facts concerning the desertion of a vessel found on the 13th December last in latitude 28.20 north, and longitude 17.51 west,[1] derelict at sea, and which was towed into the harbour of Gibraltar by the British vessel *Dei Gratia*, and there libelled by the salvors. From the log of the abandoned vessel she is supposed to be the American brigantine *Mary Celeste*, bound from New York to Genoa, and it is supposed that she hailed from New York and that her master's name was Briggs. The circumstances of the case tend to arouse grave suspicions that the master, his wife and child, and perhaps the chief mate, were murdered in the fury of drunkenness by the crew, who had evidently obtained access to the alcohol with which the vessel was in part laden. It is thought that the vessel was abandoned by the crew between the 25th day of November and the 5th day of December, and that they either perished at sea, or more likely

[1] These bearings are wrong.

A GREAT SEA MYSTERY

escaped on some vessel bound for some North or South American port or the West India Islands. When discovered the derelict vessel was thoroughly sound, with the exception of the bows, which had been damaged by some sharp instrument. She was wellfound and provisioned, and no reason for her desertion was apparent. A sword with the appearance of blood thereon was on board, and marks of blood were found on the sails. The vessel's documents and the chronometer have not been found, but almost the whole of the personal effects of the master and his wife and child and of the crew were discovered in a good condition, and books, trinkets, gold lockets and female wearing apparel of superior quality were left untouched in the cabin. The log was complete to noon of the 24th of November. Many other details concerning the matter are in the possession of the Department, and will be furnished on application if necessary."

SOME THEORIES

To this theory of mutiny which seems to have been favoured by official, but not by unofficial, opinion, there are of course some obvious objections. The first is one which time alone could establish or convict. What became of the mutineers? Granting that, their crime accomplished, they left the *Mary Celeste*, where did they go? If they boarded a passing vessel they would have found some difficulty in assuming the guise of distressed mariners. They would have had to supply full particulars of themselves, of their ship, of their reason for abandoning her, and of the fate of Captain Briggs and the mate; nor, in view of the unusually fine weather which had lately prevailed, would they have found a tale of storm and shipwreck sufficiently plausible for their purpose. Surely, too, you would suppose, they would at least have taken the precaution of scuttling the *Mary Celeste* before they left her; for a more awkward piece of evidence than such a floating conundrum could scarcely be imagined. Moreover, when

55

A GREAT SEA MYSTERY

the vessel which they boarded reached port, they would have been marked men. The news of the finding of the *Mary Celeste* created an immediate stir in the seaports of the world ; Washington, as we have seen, was on the watch for the appearance of the crew ; and there were also the underwriters, who had been bled to the extent of £1,700, and who undoubtedly would keep their eyes open for any clue to so expensive a mystery. So the mutineers could hardly have landed anywhere unidentified without the connivance of the captain ; and it is most unlikely that any captain would have taken the risk of screening them.

The mutiny theory was perhaps just tenable at Gibraltar a few weeks after the arrival of the *Mary Celeste ;* but time has almost refuted it. For the fact remains that not a single man of the *Mary Celeste's* company has ever been discovered. Plenty of people have claimed to know, or to know of, men who sailed in her, and have come forward with some story, more or less plaus-

SOME THEORIES

ible, to support their contention, but, as I
hope to show later, every one of these claims
is a plain fabrication.

A further point, which is always important
where crime is concerned, is the absence of
any apparent motive. Men as a rule do not
mutiny for the fun of the thing ; generally
they are driven to it either by greed or by the
tyranny of their commander. But Captain
Briggs was a decent, well-known, respectable
man, with a good sea reputation, not at all
the sort of person who would bully a crew
into rebellion and murder. Nor, so far as
we know, was there anything in the ship of
sufficient value to tempt cupidity to crime ;
and what there was had been left behind in
cabin and fo'c'sle. If, then, the motive behind
the supposed mutiny was neither desperation
nor greed, what was it ?

Of course these objections would have
lost much of their significance if the *Mary
Celeste* had borne obvious marks of disorder
and bloodshed, if, in fact, there was some
substantial, positive evidence to support the

A GREAT SEA MYSTERY

mutiny theory. But the ship was in perfectly good order. It is true that there were signs of her having been abandoned in a great hurry, but there was no trace of anything resembling the struggle we should expect when we reflect that the mutineers would have had to dispose of at least three and probably four persons—the Captain himself, his wife and child, and presumably the mate Richardson. The clues which suggested the mutiny theory do not really amount to very much. First, there was that curious injury to the bows which, it has been conjectured, was deliberately done in order to give the impression of a rough passage. If so, it was done remarkably badly. A child could have faked the damage better ; no one was likely to be deceived ; and even if the deception were successful, it is hard to see what would have been gained by it. Then there was the cutlass, which seemed a very likely clue until Dr. Patron's analysis proved that the stains on its blade were rust and not blood ; and there were

SOME THEORIES

those doubtful spots of blood on the deck, which were about as plentiful as a cut finger might have caused. The other so-called clues—the deep cut (as though from the blow of an axe) on the starboard top gallant-rail, the displaced hatch, the broached barrel of alcohol, and the absence of the ship's register, manifest, bills of lading and chronometer, may have meant anything—or nothing very much ; in any case, as evidence in support of the mutiny theory, their value is very questionable.

The other opinion that prevailed at Gibraltar was voiced by Captain Shufeldt in the report which he drew up after examining the *Mary Celeste*. He rejected the mutiny theory altogether, believing that the ship was probably abandoned without due cause in a moment of panic. This was certainly a more likely explanation than the other, though his suggestion that she might have sprung a leak in a gale is open to two serious objections. The first is that during the weeks when she was crossing the Atlantic

A GREAT SEA MYSTERY

there was no gale, the weather, on the contrary, being unusually fine for the time of year. The second is that everyone who examined the *Mary Celeste* at Gibraltar was agreed that she was perfectly staunch, whereas, if she had sprung a leak, some trace of it would surely have been visible in the course of the close inspection which was made.

For some time the hope persisted, both in Gibraltar and in the United States, that Captain Briggs, his wife and child, and the crew of the *Mary Celeste* would turn up ; or, at least, that some ship would arrive in port with news which would supply a clue to the mystery. But the weeks passed, and nothing happened ; and in the absence of any authentic explanation the legends began.

CHAPTER V

THE STORY OF HABAKUK JEPHSON

IN January, 1884, the *Cornhill Magazine* published as its first article a contribution entitled " J. Habakuk Jephson's Statement," which at once attracted considerable attention, especially among those who were already acquainted with the story of the *Mary Celeste*.

The " Statement " began with an account of the finding of the " *Marie* " *Celeste* by the crew of the *Dei Gratia* in latitude 38° 20′ N., longitude 17° 15′ W., and of the subsequent proceedings at Gibraltar. This account, which is given in the form of an extract from a Gibraltar newspaper, ends on a note of bewilderment : the ship was absolutely sound, her crew was missing, her boats were present and undamaged. The extract is full of errors. The *Marie Celeste* [1]

[1] I give Dr. Jephson's spelling throughout this account.

A GREAT SEA MYSTERY

is described as a brigantine of 170 tons burden, the property of Messrs. White, Russell & White, of Boston. She was sailing from Boston to Lisbon, under the command of Captain J. W. Tibbs, with a crew of seven hands, including a black cook and two coloured seamen. Besides Captain Tibbs' wife and child, the ship carried three passengers—Dr. Habakuk Jephson, who purports to be the author of the account, a Mr. J. Harton, who was a young accountant, and a Mr. Septimius Goring, a half-caste gentleman from New Orleans.

At the time of writing Dr. Jephson, apparently believing that he was about to be stricken down by paralysis, conceived it to be his duty to society to disclose what he knew of the mysterious affair of the *Marie Celeste*. He began his narrative with the information that some years previously, while serving as a doctor during the American Civil War, he had been seriously wounded; taken to a plantation close to the battlefield, he had been nursed back to health by an old

HABAKUK JEPHSON

negress. On his recovery and departure this woman presented him with a queer, black stone, shaped like a human ear, as a parting gift.

Seven or eight years later Jephson, having worked himself almost to a breakdown, was offered and accepted a passage to Lisbon in the *Marie Celeste*, joining her on October 12th, 1872, when she lay in Boston harbour. During the ensuing voyage he kept a diary, from which he quotes frequently in his " Statement." Mr. Goring, the quadroon, who occupied the cabin next to his, soon became the object, first of his curiosity, later of his suspicions, and although the two men became pretty friendly on the surface, Jephson felt that there was something wrong with his fellow-passenger. Goring had a horrible physical peculiarity, for all the fingers of his right hand were missing. He seemed to have a smattering of seamanship, and on several occasions, looking through a chink in the bulkhead dividing the cabins, Jephson saw him poring over charts. He would often

A GREAT SEA MYSTERY

talk with the black men in the crew, which was curious, since half-castes and negroes are not generally friendly.

However, until October 22nd nothing occurred to arouse more than the most intangible of suspicions. At 4.40 on the afternoon of that day Jephson, who had left his cabin a short while before and gone on deck to get some fresh air, heard a sudden explosion, and going below found that Goring, while cleaning his revolver, had accidentally discharged it. The bullet had passed through the bulkhead into the doctor's cabin and must have traversed the exact spot where Jephson's head would have rested, had he, in accordance with his custom at that hour, been lying in his bunk. Goring, of course, was full of apologies, was much upset by the mishap, and expressed profound relief at the doctor's escape.

This affair was disquieting, but worse was to follow. At eleven o'clock that night Captain Tibbs appeared in Jephson's cabin with the startling news that his wife and

HABAKUK JEPHSON

child were nowhere to be seen. A search
was at once made, without result, and in the
absence of a clue of any kind Jephson concluded that the child must have fallen overboard and that the mother, in trying to save
her, had lost her balance and followed.

The Captain, prostrated with grief, kept
his cabin the whole of the next two days.
On the third day Jephson again heard an
explosion, and rushing below found the
Captain lying dead in his cabin, a pistol by
his side, his brains blown out, and the
sinister quadroon standing over him. Goring
said that he had arrived a few seconds before
Jephson ; it was, he sadly explained, a plain
case of suicide during the agony of bereavement.

Three of the *Marie Celeste's* company were
thus accounted for. The mate now took
command and moved into the Captain's
cabin.

Nothing further of any significance happened until October 31st, when, as Jephson
was lying in his bunk, the door opened very

A GREAT SEA MYSTERY

softly, and through the slowly widening crack a fingerless hand appeared, followed a moment later by a head. It was Goring. Startled by the horrible expression on the quadroon's face, Jephson sprang up from his bunk ; whereupon Goring hastened to explain that he was suffering from toothache and had come to ask for some laudanum. With this excuse Jephson was perforce satisfied, and thought little more of the incident.

A few days later he was talking to the third passenger, Harton, and in the course of conversation showed him the curious stone which the old negress had given him during the Civil War. As he was displaying it, Goring happened to come up, and catching sight of the stone, expressed the greatest interest and surprise. He took it to show to one of the black seamen, who, on seeing it, broke into an excited babble of talk. A moment later Goring came back with it, and, remarking that it seemed to be an object of no value, made as though to throw it overboard, when to Jephson's surprise the black

HABAKUK JEPHSON

man sprang forward, took the stone away from the quadroon and returned it to its owner with every mark of respect.

About a week later Jephson's Diary mentions the heat, which was unusually oppressive for the latitude, in which, as he imagined, they were sailing. On the same date land was sighted, but instead of the expected coast of Portugal they saw, on drawing nearer, a line of reef in front of a great stretch of sandy waste. The mate was dumbfounded, as well he might be, asserting that someone must have tampered with his instruments, and that the land they saw was not Portugal but the mainland of Africa.

At this point the Diary ends, and Jephson falls back on his recollection of events. That evening the ship was hove-to not very far from the shore, to stand by until morning, when a new course would be set. Shortly before midnight, when Jephson was in his cabin, a message was brought to him that Goring wished to see him on deck and that the matter was important. On going up, he

A GREAT SEA MYSTERY

was seized from behind, overpowered, and bound by Goring and the black seamen, and threatened with instant death if he uttered a sound to warn the other white men aboard. As he lay trussed and helpless on the deck, he noticed close by the body of young Harton, who had been strangled ; and Goring, observing the doctor's horror, was good enough to explain that if he had had his way Jephson would have shared Harton's fate, but that unhappily the black sailors would not allow the owner of the little black stone to be killed.

Goring then began signalling over the side with a lamp, and presently two boats appeared out of the night and a crowd of negroes swarmed aboard the brig. They bundled Jephson into one of the boats, which they then put about as though to make the shore again ; but, after rowing a short distance, the oarsmen stood by, and Jephson, looking back to the *Marie Celeste*, saw to his rage and grief that the bound bodies of the white men aboard her were being thrown

HABAKUK JEPHSON

into the sea. A little later the ship was abandoned, to drift north to the spot where, some days later, she was found by the *Dei Gratia*. The negroes, taking to their boats once more, rowed to land.

The whole party now marched some miles to a large village, which was evidently the headquarters of the tribe that had captured Jephson. On arrival they took him through narrow lanes to a temple where he saw an immense stone idol, perfect save that it lacked one ear. Needless to say, Jephson's stone was none other than the missing piece, broken off and stolen many years before. Amid immense enthusiasm the ear was fitted to the idol, and Jephson was escorted with pomp to moderately comfortable quarters in the village. But although, as he asserts, he was regarded by the natives as a sort of god, a careful watch was kept over him so that escape was impossible, and he was forced to stay on in the village for some weeks as an honoured prisoner. On one occasion Goring paid him a visit and explained that

A GREAT SEA MYSTERY

revenge had been his motive for doing away with the crew and passengers of the *Marie Celeste*. Both his mother, who had been a slave, and his wife, had suffered grievous wrongs at the hands of white men, and he had sworn vengeance on the entire white race. He had been the undetected author of several mysterious murders in the United States. Finally, he had resolved to go to Africa and, finding an opportunity for pursuing his vendetta aboard the *Marie Celeste*, he had first thrown Mrs. Tibbs and her child over the side, then had shot the captain, and tried unsuccessfully to shoot Jephson himself. At length, with the help of the black crew and a little dirty work among the ship's instruments, he had altered the brig's course and brought her to the coast of Africa. Jephson's life, of course, had been spared through his possession of the idol's missing ear. The idol, Goring explained, was a portion of the sacred stone of Mecca, which the ancestors of the tribe had carried away with them from Arabia and which succeeding genera-

HABAKUK JEPHSON

tions, although lapsed into paganism, treated with increasing veneration. One day, however, a native had broken off and stolen one of the idol's ears ; he had fled from the village with it, and had eventually reached the United States, where all trace of him was lost. This mutilation was regarded as a fearful calamity, every misfortune which subsequently overtook the village being set to its account. Accordingly, when Jephson arrived with the missing ear, he was hailed as a saviour by the population.

It was through Goring that Jephson was at last enabled to make his escape. The quadroon had not the smallest desire to do a white man a good turn, but he recognised in Jephson a serious obstacle to his ambition to become the ruler of the tribe, and, at the same time, did not dare to put him out of the way by violence. So one night he smuggled the doctor out of the village and arranged for him to be put in a sailing-boat, piloted through the surf, and then left to make his voyage alone. After a few days at sea he

A GREAT SEA MYSTERY

was picked up by the *Monrovia*, one of the British and African Steam Navigation Company's ships, and taken on to Liverpool. He never spoke of his adventures, even to his family, being convinced that if he told the truth no one would believe him.

Such was Habakuk Jephson's story, and a good many people who had heard of the finding of the *Mary Celeste* welcomed it as the genuine solution to the mystery. Obviously, however, it is pure fiction. Apart from discrepancies too numerous to need mentioning, Jephson's figures, names and dates are all wrong. He makes the *Mary Celeste* sail from Boston for Lisbon instead of New York for Genoa, and supplies her with three passengers whom she neither did nor could accommodate, and a crew of negroes in place of her Germans. But such points are not worth labouring. Some time after the appearance of the story in the *Cornhill*, it transpired that the author was no less eminent a writer than the creator of Sherlock Holmes ; and Sir Arthur Conan

HABAKUK JEPHSON

Doyle later included " Habakuk Jephson's Statement " in a volume of short stories entitled *The Captain of the Polestar*. He must have read, or been told, of the baffling affair of the *Mary Celeste*, and, making use of as much of the facts as served his purpose, had allowed his imagination to do the rest. At least, he produced an " explanation " which makes an excellent story.

It is unfortunate that the anonymity under which he wrote, and the fact that he took as the framework of his tale a real ship and a real occurrence, should have led to misconception ; so that he cannot avoid the doubtful honour of being the pioneer of the many imaginary solutions which were later to appear in print.

CHAPTER VI

" SOLUTIONS "

FOR some years after the appearance of " Habakuk Jephson's Statement," little was heard of the *Mary Celeste*, though at intervals the story was re-told in some British or American magazine.[1] As the narrators, following the example of Sir Arthur Conan Doyle, were often tempted to supply fresh particulars out of their imaginations, the public mind can hardly be blamed if it became a little hazy about the facts.

We may place in rather a different category two " fake " solutions which appeared in the early years of this century.

The first of these was published in a London daily paper and was supplied by a

[1] As *Chambers's Journal*, October, 1904, *McClure's Magazine*, May, 1905, the *Overland Monthly*, November, 1906.

"SOLUTIONS"

Mr. R. E. Greenhough. He stated that in 1904 or 1905, while serving as an apprentice in the Swansea barque *Ardorinha*, bound for Chili, he was one of a party put ashore to fetch sand from a group of tiny islands known as St. Paul's rocks. The party, on landing, came across a skeleton, propped up against a rock, with a bottle near by filled with discoloured paper, which when taken out was found to be covered with writing. As this was in a foreign language which no one could understand, no further attention was paid to it. Mr. Greenhough, however, kept the paper, and many years later found someone to decipher and translate it.

The writing was in German, and Mr. Greenhough gave some extracts from it :

" I am dying. My ship struck these rocks at dawn three days ago. She sank immediately. Only I of all her crew reached the shore alive. There is no water ; I am dying of thirst.

" It has been a voyage of disaster. . . .

A GREAT SEA MYSTERY

killed in the engine-room. Three deaths in two days. Then came the poison on the seventh day out.

" Chronometer had run down. In my agony I forgot to wind. Only one on ship. It was the final catastrophe. Ship helpless. Too weak to get steam on boilers. And so for three days we lay.

" Knew must ask assistance to take us to Gibraltar for crew. That was ruin. Ship not insured. If English found cargo it was prison and confiscation.

" Managed to get steam to give steerage way. I headed for Lisbon. Early morning sighted small brig becalmed. Mate said, ' Take her crew.' It was the Devil's voice.

" Went aboard. Captain asked why we came. His wife and child were with him. It was hard. It would have been easy without the woman. But the mate got behind the captain, he and two others, and threw him. His wife fainted. Then we pointed pistols. Crew went into boat

"SOLUTIONS"

quietly. One man shot. He fell into the sea. . . .

" We left no one on board. The brig was called *Marie Celeste*. Would to God I had never seen her. Then the child would be yet alive. I cannot forget the child."

Here is good, full-blooded melodrama—a mystery ship, an unlawful cargo, death in the engine-room, poison, piracy, murder and shipwreck. The story rings so false that even if it were supported by proper evidence, which it is not, we should find it difficult to believe.

A " solution " of a like kind appeared in the *Nautical Magazine* of December, 1913. This time the author was a Russian, Captain Lukhmanoff, who claimed to have had the story from an old Greek sailor, Demetrius Specioti. Demetrius told him that he had been a saloon-keeper in Boston and had shipped in the *Mary Celeste* under an assumed name. During the voyage the brigantine, which he described as a long, sharp,

A GREAT SEA MYSTERY

black ship with rakish stem and masts, was unlucky enough to fall in with a pirate—pirates, of course, were so plentiful in the middle Atlantic during the 'seventies of last century !—and her crew had been impressed to replace fever casualties. The fever had continued to rage until Captain Briggs, his wife and child, and nearly all the hands succumbed to it. Finally, at the very moment when Demetrius and the men from the *Mary Celeste* had risen and were despatching their captors, the pirate was run down by an Italian steamer. Demetrius was the sole survivor. The particulars he (or Captain Lukhmanoff) gives are throughout so inaccurate and improbable as to stamp the story at once as fiction.

While we are dealing with the more extravagant of the faked solutions I may mention that I have been sent a photograph of a message in cipher, which arrived some years ago at the office of the *Gibraltar Chronicle*. It was accompanied by a letter from one Ramon Alvarado, of Cincinnati, Ohio, dated

"SOLUTIONS"

August 10th, 1909, which informed the newspaper that the key to the mystery of the *Mary Celeste* was to be found in the cipher message. This is apparently in some form of shorthand, but so far no one has been successful in decoding it. It is perhaps permissible to add that no one is recommended to waste very much time on it.

Nothing, however, was so fantastic as the explanation which appeared as recently as September, 1926, in the *British Journal of Astrology*, and which gave the entire episode of the *Mary Celeste* a mystical significance, connecting it, by processes of reasoning beyond the power of ordinary human understanding, with the Great Pyramid of Gizeh, the lost continent of Atlantis and the British Israel movement. The article is really only of interest as illustrating the nonsense which people with bees in their bonnets will solemnly set down in writing for other people with bees in their bonnets as solemnly to read.

CHAPTER VII

MORE SOLUTIONS

IN July, 1913, the *Strand Magazine* published what purported to be a complete and veracious account of the *Mary Celeste*. In fact, it was both incomplete and highly inaccurate, but it is worth mentioning, not for its merits, but because it elicited a number of interesting suggestions from various eminent authors, and was, I believe, directly responsible for introducing the story of Abel Fosdyk, with which I shall deal in the next chapter.

The writer in the *Strand* gave the Captain's name as Griggs, and the brigantine's as *Marie Celeste ;* he described her as a vessel of five hundred tons, increased the number of her crew and passengers to the sinister figure of thirteen, and so on. Moreover, presumably in order to make a better maga-

MORE SOLUTIONS

zine story of the affair, he introduced a great deal of quite imaginary dialogue, principally between the Captain of the *Dei Gratia*, to whom he gives the name of Boyce, and his mate.

The account ends by setting the problems with which Sir Arthur Conan Doyle coped so successfully in " Habakuk Jephson's Statement " ; given a ship found on the high seas, derelict but in perfect condition, what can have happened to force her crew to leave her ? And, more curious still, how *did* they leave her if none of her boats was missing ? That, indeed, was the crux of the matter, for the whole problem would be immensely simplified if it could be established that the crew got away in a boat. Sir Arthur, of course, disposed of the difficulty by producing, first, a murderous quadroon, and secondly, a swarm of African negroes who conveniently despatched the white survivors, and then decamped in their canoes with Dr. Jephson and the black crew.

The *Strand Magazine* now invited fresh

A GREAT SEA MYSTERY

answers to these questions from its readers and contributors. It obtained them from— among others—three distinguished novelists. The first of these, Mr. Barry Pain, inclined to a theory, somewhat similar to Captain Lukhmanoff's tale, of a strange vessel, the crew of which was so thinned by fever that not enough men were left to work the ship. Brought to this pass they sighted the *Mary Celeste*, boarded her, and at pistol point impressed her crew. But, as we have re-marked, the explanation has its weak points. Even in the 'seventies of last century such high-handed practices were unusual, parti-cularly on the great steamer routes, and, unless the guilty vessel subsequently foundered (as did Captain Lukhmanoff's) more would have been heard of the matter when eight indignant sailors, not to mention Mrs. Briggs, finally arrived in port.

Mr. H. A. Vachell's imagination ran to a more fantastic solution. He suggested a submarine explosion of a volcanic character, through which a noxious gas was discharged.

MORE SOLUTIONS

The *Mary Celeste* became enveloped in its fumes, which created so raging a thirst that the entire company flung themselves overboard and perished.

Finally, Mr. Arthur Morrison supplied the story, complete with details, of " Holy Joe," a madman who destroyed crew and passengers, one by one, with surprising skill and dexterity. Some he slew by putting poison in their coffee, others by creeping up behind them and felling them to the ground. After consigning their bodies to the ocean, he leaped overboard himself, leaving the *Mary Celeste* to continue on her course unmanned.

But these, of course, are sheer conjectures. They attempt to tell merely what *might* have happened, not what *did* happen. Our next " solution " is more pretentious.

CHAPTER VIII

THE STORY OF ABEL FOSDYK

FOUR months after the eminent novelists had made their incursion into the debate, the *Strand Magazine* published a lengthy contribution which claimed to give the genuine explanation of the mystery of the *Mary Celeste*. It was sent in by a Mr. Howard Linford, the head master of a private school in Hampstead, and he prefaced it with a short account of how the material came into his hands.

Until recently, he wrote, he had had in his service a man of the name of Abel Fosdyk, whom his father had engaged in 1874 on the recommendation of a friend who came across the man at the Surrey Commercial Dock. This Fosdyk was a queer customer, quite well-educated, and a bit of a linguist. He had been a sailor and obviously had knocked about the world a good

84

STORY OF ABEL FOSDYK

deal, but was reticent about his past history He stayed in Mr. Linford's employment for some years, indeed, for the rest of his life, and a short time before his death told his master that the facts about *Mary Celeste* would be found in three old boxes of papers that were among his possessions. Beyond vaguely conjecturing that *Mary Celeste* was the name of some woman who had played a part in Fosdyk's life, Mr. Linford thought little more of the matter ; indeed, after the man's death, he did not even trouble to look into the boxes, until one day he happened to read the article in the *Strand Magazine* of July, 1913, about a derelict with a name which had a familiar ring to him. Then, remembering what Fosdyk had told him, he opened the boxes, inside which he found a mass of papers, roughly in the form of a diary, and mostly relating to the ship *Mary Celeste*. Out of this material he extracted the story which was published in the *Strand Magazine* of November, 1913.

In the autumn of 1872, the narrative began,

A GREAT SEA MYSTERY

Fosdyk had found it necessary, for private reasons which the diary did not disclose, to leave America hurriedly and secretly. He had accordingly persuaded an acquaintance of his, Captain Briggs, to ship him as steward in his vessel the *Mary Celeste*, although his name was not to be shown on the ship's books.

After leaving New York, the *Mary Celeste* ran into fearful weather. That autumn— and Mr. Linford claims to be able to corroborate the statement—was notable for the violent storms which raged across the Atlantic, and from the middle of October to the middle of November the *Mary Celeste* struggled with a gale of wind and mountainous seas. The strain upon the crew, and especially upon the Captain, became almost unbearable. Briggs spent night after night on deck in sleepless vigil, and to add to his anxiety, his wife, who was making the voyage with him and was usually an excellent sailor, suffered severely from seasickness. His nerves were worn ragged ; he grew moody

STORY OF ABEL FOSDYK

and irritable and liable to flare up at a moment's provocation, then to relapse once more into profound depression.

At last the weather cleared a little, but the Captain's temper seemed to become more uncontrolled than before. Fosdyk records a curious occurrence during this lull in the storms. A capsized ship was sighted, floating bottom upwards, with some human bodies adhering to the keel. The mate, who put off in a boat to investigate, found that with one exception the bodies were corpses. The one living man they took off with some difficulty, brought back to the *Mary Celeste* and doctored. But, after lingering for a few days, he died. This incident, however, seems to have no connection with the disaster which was impending.

A few days after the finding of the capsized ship the foul weather returned, and held until the *Mary Celeste* must have been not far from the Azores. Then occurred a trivial event which was to have the most tragic consequences. Mrs. Briggs had

A GREAT SEA MYSTERY

brought with her on the voyage her daughter, a little girl of about seven. One day this child, who was known to all on board as " Baby," was seen by her father and Fosdyk climbing on the bowsprit and in imminent danger of falling into the sea. Fosdyk pulled her back to safety, but Captain Briggs, badly scared, lost his temper and boxed her ears with unnecessary violence. The child burst into tears and ran off, crying bitterly. Presently the Captain felt some remorse for his harsh treatment of her and, partly to make amends and partly to keep her out of harm's way, ordered the carpenter to rig up in the bows of the ship a little gangway where " Baby " could sit in safety. It was made out of an old door, or the top of a trestle table, with a balustrade round it ; it was fixed to the timber on either side of the bows, and was called by the crew " Baby's quarterdeck," because, when the weather was fine, the child would sit there by the hour and hail imaginary vessels.

It happened one morning at breakfast,

STORY OF ABEL FOSDYK

when the *Mary Celeste* was very close to the
Azores, that the captain and the mate had a
dispute. The captain was fond of alluding
to an old affair, from which the mate had
not emerged very creditably, when a man
had fallen into the sea and he had failed to go
to his assistance. On this occasion at breakfast, when the Captain harked back to the
subject, the mate excused his action on the
ground that he was fully dressed when the
accident occurred and could not swim in his
clothes. This explanation seemed to rile
the Captain beyond reason. The point was
argued at length and with some heat, the
Captain repeating over and over again, " So
a man can't swim in his clothes ? " The
mate was quite willing to drop the subject,
and Mrs. Briggs did her best to pacify her
husband, but at length, getting up, he vowed
that he would swim round the ship there and
then, fully dressed. Nothing that his wife
or his crew could do or say would move him
from his purpose, but when it was clear that
he was set on having his swim, two of the

89

A GREAT SEA MYSTERY

men volunteered to accompany him. So the three of them lowered themselves into the water, while the others—the mate and Fosdyk, Mrs. Briggs, " Baby " and the rest of the crew—went up into the bows to watch, and either sat upon or leaned against " Baby's quarterdeck."

The swim began, and the swimmers were just passing under the stern and round the ship, when one of the men in the water let out a fearful yell. The spectators on board at once leaned over the side to see what had happened, and under their weight the make-shift little platform tore loose from its fastenings and carried them all into the sea.

Fosdyk had a fearful struggle under water with someone who clung to him with the desperation of a drowning man, and when at last he broke away and came to the surface, gasping for breath, he found himself at some little distance from the ship. He could not see any of the others except one man, hanging on to the end of the broken platform, which was still suspended from the

STORY OF ABEL FOSDYK

bows by a single strand of rope. Marking
Fosdyk, the man shouted to him to look out
for a shark which was between the Captain
and the ship. Hardly had he spoken than
a shark shot out from the port side of the
Mary Celeste and swam swiftly in the direction of Fosdyk; providentially, however, it
passed him and disappeared.

Fosdyk began to swim as fast as he could
towards the ship when suddenly the rope,
which still secured the end of " Baby's
quarterdeck " to the ship, gave, and the
whole erection crashed into the sea, bringing
down with it and striking on the head the
man who was clinging to it. It now formed
a tolerably good raft, on to which Fosdyk
lost no time in climbing. The unconscious
body of the other man already lay across
it.

Fosdyk was not aware that when the
platform went over the side it had carried
with it everyone left in the *Mary Celeste*,
and for a while he tried to attract the attention of someone on board. To his dismay

91

A GREAT SEA MYSTERY

no answer came, and he was about to attempt to climb up the ship's side when there was a puff of wind and the brig veered off, leaving the two men behind. The weather was very fine and calm, and for some hours the brigantine and the raft drifted along in company, though at an increasing interval. Later in the day the other man died, without recovering consciousness, and Fosdyk was left alone. Without food or water he drifted about for several days, being ultimately washed ashore somewhere on the northwest coast of Africa. He was picked up in an exhausted condition and, as soon as he was sufficiently recovered, made his way to Marseilles, where he fell ill and underwent a serious operation.

Fosdyk's story was accepted by a large number of people as authentic, and even in recent years I have found the belief prevailing that the whole mystery had been cleared up in the *Strand Magazine ;* so that it is worth while to examine the narrative.

As I have already said, the heart of the

STORY OF ABEL FOSDYK

puzzle lies in the presence of the boats and the absence of the crew. How they left the ship, in fact, is a bigger enigma than why they left it. Fosdyk gets over the difficulty by the device of " Baby's quarterdeck." Having sent the Captain and two of his men for a swim, he congregates the remainder on this flimsy platform and tips it over into the sea. By virtue of this same simple structure, he is able to claim the additional merit of explaining what no one else has ever accounted for satisfactorily, those curious and baffling marks on the bows of the ship.

Yet the story, as I shall hope to show, is a forgery. Let me begin by admitting that Fosdyk spells the ship's name properly and describes her correctly as a brigantine, two small points on which the previous article in the *Strand* went astray. On the other hand, he greatly exaggerates her tonnage, putting it at 600 instead of 282, which is the true figure. He tells us that she carried thirteen people, whereas the right number was ten. He gives the names of most of the company,

A GREAT SEA MYSTERY

but with the exception of the Captain and Mrs. Briggs, the names he gives are incorrect ; nor do his descriptions of the crew tally with the facts, for he turns our four Germans, or German-Americans, into Anglo-Saxons. He says that he shipped as steward, but the real steward was Edward Head ; and " Baby," who, by his account, was of an age to clamber about the bowsprit, was actually a child of two !

These discrepancies are big enough by themselves to stamp the tale as an invention, and any doubts that may remain vanish when we come a little closer to the story. Fosdyk's dates, where he gives them, are hopelessly wide of the mark. He refers to the storms which buffeted the *Mary Celeste* between the middle of October and the middle of November, whereas she did not clear from New York until November 2nd, and may not have sailed until a few days later. The storms themselves are as fictitious as the rest of the tale ; nearly all the people who examined the *Mary Celeste* in Gibraltar

94

STORY OF ABEL FOSDYK

harbour were agreed that she was in perfect
condition and could not have met with very
rough weather ; while the *Dei Gratia*, crossing the Atlantic almost in her wake, reported
an exceptionally fine passage.

When we look at the story of the disaster,
we find it so fantastic that, even if all of
Fosdyk's facts that can be verified were
true, which they are not, we should remain
incredulous. It is not very likely that any
captain, even if his nerves were in a bad state,
would want or be allowed by his men to go
for a swim in the middle of the Atlantic
with his clothes on ; the overthrow of ten
people in the collapse of so small a platform
as " Baby's quarterdeck " is a little too convenient to be convincing ; and the idea that
a man could drift in a clumsy raft, without
sail or oar or food or water, from the Azores
to the African Coast, and survive the experience, is merely ridiculous. The narrative is full of weaknesses such as these, and
this is perhaps the reason—no other appears
—why Fosdyk chose to carry his secret with

95

A GREAT SEA MYSTERY

him to the grave rather than risk the ridicule of a sceptical public.

Finally, I may remark that either Fosdyk must have forgotten his sea jargon, or else that Mr. Linford, after carefully expurgating any expression of a nautical turn, must have substituted his own wording. We find such phrases as " No boat of her size," " We heaved to," " Got over quite a lot of ground," and " Had prepared the storm fore and aft mainsail." Without being so outspoken as the retired mariner whose comment on the story after reading it was, " The fellow who wrote that doesn't know a poopdeck from a jib down-haul," we may observe that these are the kind of trifles that betray.

CHAPTER IX

THE STORY OF TRIGGS

ON September 24th, 1924, a leading London newspaper announced, with appropriate headlines, that the problem of the *Mary Celeste* was at last solved, and that it was in a position to lay before its readers the true explanation of what it described as " the classic sea mystery." This it was enabled to do through the agency of Captain H. Lucy of the Royal Naval Reserve, a sailor well known and highly respected in the shipping circles of the Mediterranean and the East.

Captain Lucy told the correspondent who visited him that many years before, when he was mate of the *Island Princess*, cruising in the South Seas, one of the crew was a man named Triggs, whom he had met at Melbourne and to whom he had given the job

A GREAT SEA MYSTERY

of bo'sun of the Kanaka crew. Lucy and Triggs were shipmates for about three months, and at different times during their association the latter divulged piecemeal and " under oath " the most extraordinary tale.

Triggs—Captain Lucy did not believe this to be the man's real name—declared that he had signed on as bo'sun aboard the *Mary Celeste* in the autumn of 1872. She made a good passage across the Atlantic and was about twenty-four hours' sailing distance from the coast of Spain or Portugal when, about midday, a steamer was sighted, rolling heavily, with empty decks, and by all appearances, derelict. The sea being calm, Captain Briggs ordered the mate, Triggs and four of the men to row over to her, as something of value might have been left aboard. When they reached the steamer, they were unable to read her name, which had been rusted away by salt water, but ascertained that she belonged to the Port of London. Boarding her, they discovered in the purser's cabin a big iron safe which they could not open.

THE STORY OF TRIGGS

Triggs and two of the men were sent back to the *Mary Celeste* for the carpenter and his tools, and on their return the safe was forced. Inside it was £3,500 in gold and silver.

Triggs went back to the *Mary Celeste* with the news, and Captain Briggs at once accompanied him to the derelict. There he and the mate had a private confabulation, as a result of which the Captain gave orders for the money to be taken across to the brig in the derelict's boats and for the steamer's watercocks to be opened, as she was a danger to shipping.

So the derelict was scuttled, and, on the return of the men to the *Mary Celeste*, the treasure was divided. The Captain took £1,200, the mate £600, the second mate £400, and Triggs himself £300 ; the balance of £1,000 was distributed among the crew.

So far so good. But now the question was raised : was this satisfactory little transaction quite legal ? The Captain thought not, and no one was sufficiently certain of the law to

A GREAT SEA MYSTERY

contradict him. After some discussion, it was decided to take no risks, to send the *Mary Celeste* to join the derelict at the bottom of the sea, and to make for Cadiz in the steamer's boats. There they would pose as a shipwrecked crew and, having satisfied all inquiries, make off with the gold. But, just as they were about to execute this plan, they were spoken by a passing vessel. This was awkward for them. Suspicion would certainly be aroused were a brig to be seen sinking for no apparent reason on a calm day. So they resolved instead to leave the *Mary Celeste* just as she was. First of all, they painted on the steamer's boats the name of a schooner from London ; and then, embarking in them with the money and some provisions, reached Cadiz, fifty miles away, on the following morning. There they played their part of distressed mariners, pitching a fine tale about their schooner which, they stated, had struck a submerged wreck and gone down. The Captain spent money freely in Cadiz to support the story.

THE STORY OF TRIGGS

The conspirators then separated, the Captain and his family, the two mates and Triggs going on to Marseilles, while the rest of the crew sailed for London in a Spanish fruit ship.

Captain Lucy kept this astonishing tale to himself for forty years, and during this long reticence, he tells us, he has often smiled over the various published " solutions " to the mystery of the *Mary Celeste*.

Certainly as a survivor of the famous brigantine, Triggs at once ousted Abel Fosdyk in the popular esteem, an evening paper actually breaking out into a leading article which hailed and deplored the end of the great mystery.

Let us, however, in all fairness, subject Mr. Triggs to the same tests as have been applied to his rivals. To begin with, it may be observed that the name of the ship is spelt wrongly as the *Marie Celeste*, but that may have been the error of Captain Lucy or the printer ; then the number of the crew is given as seventeen, and their nationality

A GREAT SEA MYSTERY

as American, Danish and Norwegian. These are perhaps small matters, though it is worth noting that the real *Mary Celeste* carried no one answering to the name or description of Mr. Triggs. Still, Captain Lucy did warn us that he believed the name to be assumed, so we may allow him the benefit of the doubt.

The next point is more important. According to Triggs, the derelict was sighted about fifty miles from Cadiz, that is, somewhere in the outer waters of the Gulf of Cadiz. But, as we know, the *Mary Celeste* was found by the *Dei Gratia* a good two hundred miles from the Gulf of Cadiz. It follows, then, that between November 24th, when the last entry in the log placed the *Mary Celeste* off the Azores, and December 5th, when the *Dei Gratia* picked her up, she performed the following astounding feat : she first sailed east more than nine hundred miles on her proper course, and then, after being abandoned, turned round and drifted two hundred miles west to Cape St. Vincent

THE STORY OF TRIGGS

and north-west to the latitude where she was eventually found. She did this in ten days, during which a north or north-east wind was blowing.

Although these circumstances by themselves are quite enough to dispose of Triggs and his tale, we will carry our inquiry a little further. This derelict steamer, he would have us believe, was floating about, not in unfrequented waters, but plumb in the middle of one of the great ocean highways of the world, close to a big port and at the very gate of the Mediterranean. That, too, is remarkable. Again, the steamer's name, which by Board of Trade rule must have appeared on her bow and stern, had been rusted away in both places ; nor, apparently, was any note taken of her official number, a sure clue to her identity, which by a similar regulation must have been cut on the main beam. It is true that Captain Lucy believed Triggs to be lying when he stated that he did not know the derelict's name, and where a gentleman as credulous as Captain

A GREAT SEA MYSTERY

Lucy seems to be expresses a doubt, most of us will feel safe in professing a certainty.

Next, the derelict herself presents a problem almost as mysterious as the *Mary Celeste*. Who had abandoned her ? And why ? What became of her crew ? And what was the purser about to leave £3,500 lying in her safe when he went over the side ? To these questions, of course, no answer is given.

Then the financial aspect of the whole business is rather puzzling. Captain Briggs, we are told, went off with £1,200 as his share of the loot, out of which presumably came the hush-money disbursed at Cadiz ; so that probably in the end he did not clear much more than a thousand. Now let us look at the other side of his balance sheet. He was a man of some substance. He owned a third share of the *Mary Celeste*, not to mention any interest he may have had in a cargo valued at nearly thirty-seven thousand dollars, and in the voyage. He had a home in New England, a wife and family, a job and

THE STORY OF TRIGGS

an unblemished reputation. Yet all these
assets, tangible and intangible, he was ready
to fling away for a miserable £1,200 ; be-
coming by his action a wanderer on the face
of the earth, unable to return to his home, or
to follow his calling, or even to use his own
name. A more unlikely bargain can scarcely
be imagined, and we can be sure that, even
if Captain Briggs had fallen to it, his wife,
mindful of her son and her home, would
have had something to say.

The Captain's conduct, after deciding to
share out the money, is equally incompre-
hensible. His obvious course would have
been to scuttle the derelict, boats and all, and
sail on to Gibraltar as though nothing out of
the way had happened. But Captain Lucy
tells us that Briggs was afraid to do this lest,
on reaching Genoa, some of the men might
talk in their cups. But he does not explain
why this was more likely to happen at Genoa
than at Cadiz. Nor does he attempt to
justify the extraordinary plan which Briggs
ultimately adopted. First of all, he says,

105

A GREAT SEA MYSTERY

the men intended to scuttle the *Mary Celeste*, but later, to avoid a suspicion of foul play, they left her afloat and went off in the derelict's boats, on which they painted the name of the London schooner. They then turned up at Cadiz, presumably without papers of any kind, and with a trumpery tale of a sunken wreck. Captain Lucy appears to think that three boat-loads of alleged shipwrecked mariners can arrive at a port like Cadiz without attracting any particular attention, and that neither the British Consul, nor Lloyd's, nor the proprietors of the London schooner whose name they had borrowed, would have taken the trouble to verify their story. It is nice to think that there are such guileless people abroad, but perhaps Captain Lucy supposes that palms had been so well greased by a few hundred pounds of hush-money that neither consul, nor underwriter, nor shipowner would say a word.

Meanwhile, in order to make quite sure of setting every tongue in the Mediterranean wagging, the *Mary Celeste* was abandoned

THE STORY OF TRIGGS

in the Gulf of Cadiz, so that her ultimate discovery would be almost inevitable.

I hope I have said enough to persuade the reader that Triggs is about as genuine a witness as Abel Fosdyk. Whether the leg that was pulled was that of Captain Lucy or of the editor of the London newspaper is a matter on which I would rather not hazard an opinion.

CHAPTER X

THE STORY OF JOHN PEMBERTON

I NOW come to the latest and, in my opinion, the most plausible of all the "Solutions" to the mystery of the *Mary Celeste*. It appeared in *Chambers's Journal* for July, 1926, from the pen of Mr. Lee Kaye, who claimed to have had the story from no less an authority than the cook of the *Mary Celeste*. This man he called John Pemberton, giving his age as seventy-six, and describing him as a naval pensioner of the American Civil War. Pemberton, moreover, was not the only survivor from the crew, for Mr. Lee Kaye mentioned one Jack Dossell, the bo'sun, who died near Shrewsbury as recently as 1919.

Mr. Lee Kaye begins by giving particulars of the *Mary Celeste*, which he describes as brig-rigged, with a register of 282 tons gross.

STORY OF JOHN PEMBERTON

" She was clipper-built and had a long, low quarterdeck, with the cabin built through it to a height of six feet above the planking." Originally named the *Amazon*, she had been re-christened the *Mary Sellers*, which in turn had been corrupted to *Mary* or *Marie Celeste*. She was the property of Mr. J. H. Winchester, who chartered her to a New York Company—Bremmer Brothers—in 1867.

On September 30th she was lying in New York loading a cargo of railway timber and whale oil for Genoa, and as there was more oil than she could take in, " the Company had part-chartered an English vessel, the *Dei Gratia*, to carry the surplus." But Briggs, the captain of the *Mary Celeste*, was in a quandary. He could not complete his crew, as no one wanted to sign on in a small ship carrying so unpleasant a cargo as whale oil. With the *Dei Gratia*, however, which was a much larger vessel, the difficulty was not so great, and eventually Briggs persuaded her Master, Captain Morehouse, to transfer

A GREAT SEA MYSTERY

temporarily three of his men to the *Mary Celeste*, which now carried ten people :

Captain and Mrs. Briggs.

Mr. Hullock, mate (U.S.A.).

Jack Dossell, boatswain and carpenter (U.S.A.)

Peter Sanson (Nova Scotia).

Carl Venholdt (U.S.A.).

John Pemberton, cook (British),

and the three men from the *Dei Gratia* :

Tom Moffat (Nova Scotia).

Charlie Manning (British).

Billie Hawley (Irish).

The *Dei Gratia* had to make a first call at Queenstown, where she was to land a consignment of wines, and by arrangement between the Captains, the two ships were subsequently to keep a *rendezvous* at Santa Marta in the Azores, where Captain Briggs hoped to pick up some men, so that he could release those he had borrowed from the *Dei Gratia*.

Captain Morehouse put to sea on October 2nd, leaving the *Mary Celeste* in New York. The next day Mrs. Briggs joined her hus-

STORY OF JOHN PEMBERTON

band, bringing with her for her amusement on the voyage a piano which, much to the mate's disgust, was lashed to the cabin bulkhead, in the precise spot where he had been meaning to stow his sea-chest.

The *Mary Celeste* left New York on October 7th, and almost at once there was trouble with the crew. The ship was " very heavily sparred and slow to her helm," which meant a deal of hard work for a scratch lot of men. Moreover, the mate, Hullock, was the worst sort of slave-driver; he bullied all the men, and particularly Carl Venholdt, a burly farm-hand from Ohio who had been " shanghaied " and, until brought to submission by seasickness, resisted every attempt to make a sailor of him.

On November 1st the *Mary Celeste* ran into foul weather, and the pitching of the ship shook Mrs. Briggs's piano from its lashings. Hullock soon put the matter right, but this slight occurrence was to have the most serious consequences.

On the afternoon of November 24th, when

A GREAT SEA MYSTERY

the *Mary Celeste* was about four hundred miles north-west of the Azores, Mrs. Briggs was seated at her piano. A stiff breeze was blowing, and Peter Sanson, apparently rather a happy-go-lucky fellow, was at the wheel. Catastrophe came suddenly. The *Mary Celeste* was always slow to her helm, Peter was dreaming, and a sudden gust of wind sent the brig over on her starboard beam. Peter quickly squared her up again, but the lurch had torn the piano again from its lashings, and the heavy instrument, crashing forward, had pinned Mrs. Briggs against the bulkhead. She was fatally injured and died early the next morning.

The Captain was inconsolable ; his brain became affected by his bereavement and, unreasonably, he put most of the blame for the accident on the mate, whom he accused of having lashed the piano insecurely. The ship's company, never a happy family, was further depressed by the accident, and the men talked openly of leaving the ship at the first opportunity.

STORY OF JOHN PEMBERTON

On November 26th the Captain, whose manner had been growing more and more strange, abruptly ordered Peter Sanson to be thrown overboard. The crew naturally refused, but to satisfy the old man the piano was jettisoned instead of Peter. That evening Captain Briggs disappeared. As the mate observed, he had " gone after the piano."

With the death of the Captain discipline went to pieces. The men were thoroughly demoralised and, to keep their spirits up, Hullock plied them with rum. On November 29th, when the *Mary Celeste* was off Santa Marta in the Azores, there was a further misadventure. Venholdt, the " shanghaied " man, inflamed with drink, had a row with the mate, whom he charged with having murdered Briggs. There was a scuffle, in the course of which Hullock accidentally pushed Venholdt over the side. No attempt was made to rescue him, and he was drowned.

After all this we are not surprised to hear

A GREAT SEA MYSTERY

that when the brig drew close in to the shore and was surrounded by bumboats peddling fruit and knick-knacks, Hullock, the bo'sun and Peter Sanson seized their opportunity and left the ship. Pemberton and the three men from the *Dei Gratia* stayed on board and, when the others failed to return, determined to await the arrival of the *Dei Gratia*, according to the plan the two Captains had made at New York.

By December 4th the other ship had not appeared, so the men agreed to sail on towards Gibraltar. On the 7th they sighted and were overhauled by the *Dei Gratia*.

On hearing of the *Mary Celeste's* unfortunate voyage, Captain Morehouse had a very bright idea. The brig's crew now consisted of three of his own men and Pemberton, the cook ; in other words, her complement, with a solitary exception, had disappeared. Captain Morehouse, if he had been an honest man, would have taken her on to Gibraltar and told the truth when he arrived there. Unfortunately, he was not

114

STORY OF JOHN PEMBERTON

an honest man. (This, of course, is Mr. Lee Kaye's story, not mine.) He resolved to treat her as a derelict, to concoct a likely tale of finding her abandoned in mid-ocean, and to claim salvage. With the exception of Pemberton, who would have to be kept in the background, all the men in both vessels appeared on the *Dei Gratia's* roll, so that the risk of detection was small.

The plot succeeded admirably. At Gibraltar there was mystification, a little suspicion, perhaps, but no worse, and finally a handsome award for Morehouse and his men. As the whole company was interested in hushing up the facts, the truth never came out until the other day when Pemberton, who, presumably, had taken a share of the plunder, told it to Mr. Lee Kaye.

It must be owned that this is quite the best of all the sham solutions. Without putting too severe a strain on our credulity, Mr. Lee Kaye has succeeded in emptying (or practically emptying) the ship without lowering a boat ; and he has fortified his

A GREAT SEA MYSTERY

story with an amount of detailed information (much of which is authentic) about the *Mary Celeste*, her crew and her voyage, that quite puts to shame the efforts of Mr. Linford and Captain Lucy.

Yet in the cause of accuracy we may rejoice, though in the cause of art we may deplore, that certain obvious blemishes remain to mar this plausible creation. Always we get back to hard things like dates and facts, and the dates and facts are as fatal to Mr. Lee Kaye as they were to his predecessors.

Let us take the dates first, noting that these are given very plentifully and definitely. The *Dei Gratia*, says Mr. Lee Kaye, left New York on October 2nd; but we happen to know, on the joint authority of Lloyd's and the American Maritime Register, that she did not clear until November 11th, and may not have sailed till some days later. The *Mary Celeste*, on the other hand, sailed, not, as Pemberton would have us believe, on October 7th, but on November 7th, that is, before, and not after, the *Dei Gratia*.

STORY OF JOHN PEMBERTON

These errors can hardly be dismissed as lapses in an old man's memory ; the dates are given with confidence, and continue to be wrong throughout the story, which largely depends on them. Thus we are told that " bad weather hit *Marie Celeste* on 1st November," actually at least six days before she sailed ; and that the accident to Mrs. Briggs occurred on November 24th, when the ship was five days from the Azores, whereas the log, which was in perfectly good order, placed her close to and a little to the south of the islands on that day. So much for the dates. Now for the facts.

We can pass over such slips as the wrong spelling of Captain Morehouse's name—it appears as " Moorhouse "—and the substitution of Santa Marta for Santa Maria in the Azores. These are the kind of mistakes which, after the lapse of years, an old man's memory may betray him into making. But while such trivialities as these do not affect the story, there are plenty of serious dis-

A GREAT SEA MYSTERY

crepancies which cannot be dismissed so lightly.

For instance, Pemberton states that the cargo of the *Mary Celeste* consisted of railway timber and whale oil, and it was the presence of the latter, it will be recalled, which compelled Captain Briggs to borrow men from the *Dei Gratia.* Yet from every source of any authority, from *Lloyd's List* to the proceedings of the Vice-Admiralty Court at Gibraltar, we know that the cargo was alcohol.

Mr. Lee Kaye next gives the names of all on board, but, saving the captain and his wife, every name he gives is incorrect ; and, further, he fails to mention the Captain's child, leaving us uncertain whether the little girl departed in the bumboat with Mr. Hullock (a most unsuitable companion), or, with Mr. Pemberton as dry-nurse, went on in the ship to Gibraltar.

Finally, we are told that the *Dei Gratia* called at Queenstown, but no such call was reported by Lloyd's agent ; on the contrary,

STORY OF JOHN PEMBERTON

she was reported as spoken on November 19th in latitude 41 N., longitude 66 W.,[1] far to the south of her course, if she were making the South of Ireland, and in the same report her voyage was officially given as " New York to Gibraltar."

This accumulation of errors is so conclusive that it is scarcely necessary to dwell upon some of the lesser discrepancies in the story. But it is odd that, in addition to the harmonium in the cabin, Mrs. Briggs should have insisted on taking a piano with her;[2] and that, when Hullock bolted from the ship at the Azores, he should have neglected to take any of his possessions away with him, even leaving an unfinished letter to his wife on the cabin table. There was no evidence in favour of the rough weather to which Pemberton alludes, and the appearance of the cabin and the fo'c'sle pointed, not to a

[1] *Lloyd's List*, December 6th, 1872.

[2] The harmonium actually found in the cabin was sent back to America, and is to-day in the possession of Mr. Arthur Briggs, of New Bedford, Massachusetts.

119

A GREAT SEA MYSTERY

piecemeal abandonment of the ship, but to the sudden, hurried and simultaneous departure of all on board.

So, once more, the story dissolves under test, and we are obliged to condemn as fiction this latest and most ingenious " solution " to the mystery of the *Mary Celeste*.

CHAPTER IX

THE TRUTH

WHAT is the true explanation of the mystery? It is easy to pick holes in the conjectures or spurious solutions of other people, especially when those other people have not taken the trouble to acquaint themselves properly with the facts. But it is a much more difficult task to produce something constructive, that is, something more substantial than just another theory.

In *Mysteries of the Sea* I put forward a solution which a number of people were kind enough to approve, and which others, perfectly reasonably, regarded as too far-fetched to be permissible. My solution was suggested to me by the horrible and authentic story of the *Mary Russell*, a brig sailing from Barbadoes to Cork in 1828, whose Captain suddenly went off his head and, with the assistance of two apprentices, first bound and

A GREAT SEA MYSTERY

then butchered the greater part of his crew, only two men, both badly injured, managing to escape from him and to hide in the hold. I suggested that the presence of the harmonium and of religious books and music in the cabin of the *Mary Celeste* might possibly be the clue to a similar tragedy ; that the Captain, a man of excellent character, might have developed religious mania, and, with the strength and cunning of the homicidal lunatic, have attacked, overpowered and murdered his wife and child and crew, taking them one by one and unawares ; and that finally, the mad Captain of an empty ship, he may have recovered his senses, as homicidal maniacs generally do, and, horrified by his crimes, have thrown himself overboard.

All this was merely conjecture, of which little more could be said than that, although there was not a jot of positive evidence in its support, it roughly accounted for most of the facts as I have given them.

Since the appearance of *Mysteries of the Sea*, however, I have accumulated much

THE TRUTH

fresh material, and have had access to sources of information of the existence of which I was ignorant at the time of writing. In particular, I am indebted to Dr. Oliver Cobb, who is intimately connected with the Briggs family, to Mr. Sprague, the American Vice-Consul at Gibraltar, and to one or two other gentlemen, mostly resident in the United States, for particulars the study of which compels me to admit that my " solution " in *Mysteries of the Sea* is as valueless as these other " solutions " I have criticised. By way of amends I shall now give what I believe to be the true story.

It will have been observed that there are really two distinct, albeit connected, mysteries to be solved : why was the *Mary Celeste* abandoned ? and how, no boat being missing, was she abandoned ? and that the ingenuity of the solvers has been concentrated upon the second problem. There is more than one reason why a vessel in apparently perfect condition might be deserted by its crew ; but it is by no means so easy

A GREAT SEA MYSTERY

to explain how the crew can have left the ship if they did not go off in one of her boats. So Mr. Lee Kaye has his story of borrowed men, of bumboats at the Azores and an insurance swindle ; Captain Lucy produces a derelict whose boats are handy for his purpose ; Mr. Linford gives us the crude but convenient fiction of " Baby's quarter-deck " ; and Sir Arthur Conan Doyle disposes of the problem by murder and a couple of native canoes.

The truth, when we consider all these ingenious excursions, is rather astonishing ; for the truth is simply that the only boat which the *Mary Celeste* carried on the fateful voyage *was* missing. On this point the *Maritime Register* is explicit : " There were no boats on board when she was found " ; and if further evidence is required it is forthcoming in the records of the Admiralty Court and the United States Consular office at Gibraltar.

The fact is that the *Mary Celeste* should have carried two boats, a long-boat and a

124

THE TRUTH

yawl. Unfortunately, while the cargo was being loaded at New York and the heavy barrels of alcohol were being swung aboard, a rope gave, and two of the kegs, slipping, fell on the long-boat and damaged it so badly that it was useless. Captain Briggs reported the mishap to his agents, and asked for the boat to be replaced before he sailed ; but for some reason or other this was not done, and the *Mary Celeste* accordingly put to sea carrying only her yawl, which though able at a pinch to accommodate all her company, was of course smaller and less seaworthy than the long-boat.

I purposely refrained from mentioning earlier that when the mate of the *Dei Gratia* boarded the *Mary Celeste* he noticed at once that the yawl was missing from the stern where it had hung, and that the davits were swung out with trailing ropes. To him and to Captain Morehouse, at least, there was no mystery about the method of departure of the brigantine's crew ; they had obviously gone off in the yawl.

125

A GREAT SEA MYSTERY

All this is perfectly clear from the proceedings of the Admiralty Court, from the report of the American Consul at Gibraltar, from the statements of the owner, Captain Winchester, and from the recollection of such people as Mrs. Morehouse, widow of the Captain of the *Dei Gratia*, Dr. Cobb and Arthur Briggs, the son of Captain Briggs, who naturally familiarised himself with every detail of a story so tragically affecting his family.

It is strange that the legend that none of the boats was missing should have been so confidently and persistently repeated. Its origin is obscure. To the best of my belief, its sponsor is Sir Arthur Conan Doyle, for the legend makes its first appearance in his " Statement of Habakuk Jephson," where we are told, on the authority of the *Gibraltar Gazette* [1] of January 4th, 1874, that " The boats were intact and slung upon the davits."

---

[1] There is a newspaper with the title *Gibraltar Chronicle and Official Gazette*, but the extract quoted by Habakuk Jephson does not appear in the number named.

THE TRUTH

The others seem to have been content with slavish imitation, without attempting to verify a circumstance which undoubtedly made the better part of the mystery.

Here, then, is our first point settled beyond dispute. Our second, though less formidable, is not disposed of so easily. *Why* was the *Mary Celeste* abandoned ?

Captain Morehouse, whose opinion as a witness almost at first hand cannot be ignored, always believed that on the morning of November 25th, the *Mary Celeste* was becalmed a few miles to the north of the rugged and precipitous coast of Santa Maria in the Azores ; that a current began to drive her towards the shore ; and that the crew, in a sudden panic, took to the boat. Probably they intended to stand by and, if a breeze sprang up, to rejoin the ship ; but unfortunately they did not take the precaution of attaching the yawl by a line to the *Mary Celeste*. So, when the desired breeze came, the brigantine careered away from them and, row as strongly as they could, they were un-

A GREAT SEA MYSTERY

able to overhaul her. Captain Morehouse believed that ultimately the boat was driven ashore and beaten to pieces in the surf at the foot of the cliffs, while all those in her perished.

This view was also taken by Captain James Briggs, a brother of the missing Captain. Yet it is not altogether satisfactory. The last entry in the *Mary Celeste's* log reported fine weather, a light wind and land six miles distant. The ship might have been becalmed and drifted inshore a little later in the day, but the situation could hardly have called for such a precipitate evacuation as took place. Captain Briggs was no raw youngster, but a sailor of experience ; not the sort of man, you would suppose, to abandon his ship save in extremity, or, having ordered his men into a boat to await a favour-able breeze, to have omitted the obvious precaution of hanging out a line, so that if the breeze came, the ship could be regained.

For these reasons I am inclined to accept

THE TRUTH

the solution favoured by Dr. Cobb as the more likely.

Dr. Cobb believes that the clue to the mystery is to be found in the cargo, which, it will be remembered, consisted of 1,700 barrels of alcohol. Under normal circumstances such a cargo, if properly stowed, should be quite safe, but experts in marine insurance have expressed the view that under certain conditions gases might be generated and danger ensue. Given a sufficiently high temperature, local explosions might occur, and be followed possibly by a general explosion of the whole cargo. The result in a small ship such as the *Mary Celeste* can be imagined : the 1,700 barrels of crude alcohol would have blown her to pieces and destroyed in a moment every soul on board.

With this possibility before us, let us try to reconstruct the tragedy which befell the *Mary Celeste* on November 25th, 1872. She was a few miles from the island of Santa Maria. The weather was fine, a light wind was blowing, and we may assume that for

A GREAT SEA MYSTERY

the latitude and the time of year it was a pretty warm day. As the *Mary Celeste* slipped along, pitching slightly in the Atlantic swell, we may suppose that the quiet routine of the day was broken by a danger signal. It may be that someone noticed a smell of gas lingering round the hatches beneath which the cargo was stowed ; or possibly the alarm was given by queer rumbling noises such as in a warm climate gas, escaping from alcohol, may make when disturbed by the motion of the ship. The Captain ordered one of the hatches to be removed so that air might reach the cargo and disperse any gas that had formed. While the men were lifting the heavy hatch, there was an explosion, overturning the hatch and perhaps injuring one of the men working on it. Instantly there was alarm and possibly confusion, since at any moment a further explosion might occur and blow the ship sky high. Some of the men began to take in sail, others hurriedly to lower the yawl, the only boat the *Mary Celeste* had.

THE TRUTH

A moment later there was a second small explosion, followed by something very like a panic. There was no time for further preparation, to take in more sail, to lash the wheel, or properly to provision the boat. The Captain snatched up his chronometer and such of the ship's papers as he could quickly lay his hands upon ; someone burst open a drawer and took out a few tins of preserved meat ; and all on board without further delay tumbled over the side into the yawl. Possibly in the hurry of launching, the small boat, rather heavily laden, was capsized and all were drowned. Or perhaps they got clear of the ship. If so, their one thought was to place as much water as possible between themselves and that perilous cargo, and they rowed with desperate haste away from the *Mary Celeste*. But the minutes passed ; nothing happened ; they stopped rowing and watched. Presently the wind freshened and the brigantine ran away from them.

They may have tried to row after her and

A GREAT SEA MYSTERY

failed to reach her, or, still haunted by the fear of an explosion, have turned the yawl's head towards the distant shore of Santa Maria. We may conjecture at random their fate. They may have drawn near to the coast and been caught in the surf, the yawl dashed to pieces and ten lives lost. No trace of the boat was ever found, but the disappearance of a small boat in the wide waters of the Atlantic is a minor mystery that need not detain us.

Meanwhile the removal of the hatchway had released the gases from the hold of the *Mary Celeste*, the fresh air had poured in and, all danger past, the brigantine sailed on unmanned to her strange assignation with the *Dei Gratia* off the coast of Portugal.

This solution surely covers all the facts without overstraining our sense of probability. It explains the state of suspended routine which so puzzled the men from the *Dei Gratia*, the headlong haste with which the ship was abandoned, the overturned hatch, the barrel of alcohol which bore signs

132

THE TRUTH

of having been tampered with and which doubtless was damaged in the explosion, possibly the spots of blood upon the deck. The cutlass, which at first was believed to be a clue, was later dismissed as of no significance, the stains upon it proving on analysis to be not blood but rust ; and the cuts round the bows had probably no connection with the affair at all.

Incidentally this explanation tallies with the opinion of Captain J. H. Winchester, the principal owner, who, as soon as the news of the finding of the ship reached him, crossed the Atlantic and reached Gibraltar in time to attend the salvage proceedings. Captain Winchester died in 1912, but we have the assurance of his grandson, Mr. Winchester Noyes, that he always expressed his conviction that Captain Briggs abandoned the *Mary Celeste* under an apprehension that the cargo was on the point of exploding.[1] There are indications that he put forward the same view in private conversation at

[1] *Nautical Gazette*, December, 1913.

A GREAT SEA MYSTERY

Gibraltar and later when he had returned to the United States. He was an experienced shipmaster, and as being the derelict's principal owner, and as being intimately acquainted with her Captain, and as having had the opportunity of inspecting the ship as she lay in Gibraltar harbour, he was as qualified as anyone to pass an opinion.

CHAPTER XII

THE SEQUEL

NO account of the *Mary Celeste* would be complete without a mention of her subsequent history and disastrous end.

After the salvage proceedings at Gibraltar had closed with the award to Captain Morehouse and his men, the brigantine was handed back to its principal owner. A fresh crew was engaged—not, it is said, without some difficulty—and on March 10th, 1873, the *Mary Celeste* resumed her interrupted voyage to Genoa, under the command of Captain George W. Blatchford. At Genoa she was hove down to have her bottom surveyed, but a careful examination failed, of course, to reveal any weakness or injury that might have explained the abandonment of the ship.

On her return to America she was sold,

135

A GREAT SEA MYSTERY

and thereafter changed hands frequently and at prices well below her commercial value. Sailors are superstitious folk, and the *Mary Celeste* had become a marked ship : no one wanted to own her, or to sail in her, or to have anything to do with her.

I quote an extract out of a letter to Mr. Frederick J. Shepard, of Buffalo, from a correspondent who had happened to mention the brigantine's name to a shipowner of his acquaintance, Mr. Raphael de Florez. Mr. Florez said that he was ignorant of the details of the story, but added :

" The *Mary Celeste* was always a hoodoo ; nobody would buy her. Why, she lay for more than a year in the Erie Basin, and no one wanted her. The broker who had her for sale told me that one day a negro or mulatto called on him, said he wanted to buy a vessel of that size to put his son in the African trade. He took him along to the vessel, crossed the ferry to Brooklyn, and just as they were leaving the ferry house on the Brooklyn side the

THE SEQUEL

negro said : ' Say, Mister, what do you call this brig ? ' The broker said : ' *Mary Celeste*,' and at these words the negro, who had seemed a man of some intelligence, was filled with terror, shouted : ' Go away from me : I won't have nothing to do with her,' broke away from the man and ran back, and jumped on the ferry boat as if panic-stricken. The broker, amused that even a ' nigger,' as he called him, should balk at the name, went on more than ever convinced that she was an unlucky ship."

At the end of 1884 the *Mary Celeste* made her last voyage, leaving Boston with a cargo of general merchandise for Port-au-Prince, Haiti. On January 3rd, 1885, she ran aground on Roshell's Reef, off the Haitian coast, and became a total loss, the crew being landed at Miragoane.

Mr. Kingman Putnam, a well-known surveyor of New York and the brother of Major Putnam, the famous publisher, gave some interesting details in an article which he con-

A GREAT SEA MYSTERY

tributed to the *Nautical Gazette* of December 31st, 1913. Shortly after the wreck of the *Mary Celeste*, Mr. Putnam was instructed to go to the port of Aux Cayes, on the south coast of Haiti, to investigate the loss of the schooner *Mary L. Phipps*. Before he left several underwriters handed him the papers relating to claims received from the shippers of the cargo of the *Mary Celeste*. Their suspicions had been aroused by the fact that, a portion of the cargo consisting of ale, more bottles had been billed to a barrel than a barrel would hold ; and they asked Mr. Putnam to look into the business when he was in the neighbourhood of Miragoane.

On arriving at Port-au-Prince Mr. Putnam called on the firms to whom the merchandise carried by the *Mary Celeste* had been consigned, and was given copies of the letters they had received from the shippers at Boston. He then rode across on horseback to Miragoane, where the brigantine's crew had been landed after the wreck. There he found that Captain Parker, the master, had

138

THE SEQUEL

sold the entire cargo, which had been insured
for about $30,000, for the sum of $500 to
the United States consul, Mr. Mitchel, that
the greater part of the cargo had been successfully salved, but that, oddly enough, Mr.
Mitchel was reported to have lost money
over a transaction which ought to have
yielded him a handsome profit. Something
was certainly amiss ; and what it was soon
came to light when Mr. Putnam had a look
at the cargo.

" I opened one case that had been shipped
as cutlery and insured for $1,000. It con-
tained dog collars worth about $50. Cases
insured as boots and shoes contained shoddy
rubbers worth about 25 cents each." The
bottles of alleged ale proved on inspection
to be filled with water.

Here were all the indications of fraud.
Mr. Putnam made friends with the Captain
of a schooner lying off Miragoane and got
him to buy up some of the cases, obtaining
at the same time from Mr. Mitchel a consular invoice certifying that the goods were

A GREAT SEA MYSTERY

from the cargo of the *Mary Celeste*. The cases were then shipped and delivered to a lawyer in Boston, and matters began to move in a direction most unfavourable to as pretty a piece of barratry as had occurred for some years.

In the upshot the master of the *Mary Celeste* was indicted for barratry and conspiracy, and the shippers of the cargo were associated with him in the second charge. Further evidence being required in the form of the original letters from the shippers in the States to the consignees at Port-au-Prince, a special steamer was chartered and Mr. Putnam returned to Haiti as a Deputy-Marshal, armed with powers to subpoena witnesses and with an order for Mr. Mitchel to return with him to stand his trial.

The subpoenas, though of doubtful value in a country which lay, strictly speaking, beyond the jurisdiction of the United States, enabled Mr. Putnam to extract the required documents from the merchants of Port-au-Prince. From there the steamer took Mr.

140

THE SEQUEL

Putnam on to Miragoane, where a Haitian general came on board with the news that the delinquent consul, Mr. Mitchel, was about to take to the woods. However, he assured Mr. Putnam that all would be well, for the President of the Black Republic, anxious to oblige, had instructed him to take a file of soldiers and put Mr. Mitchel, willy-nilly, aboard the steamer.

Unfortunately this neighbourly offer was a little too arbitrary to be accepted. The steamer, the *Saxon*, sailed under the British flag ; Mr. Mitchel was an American citizen ; and, the *Saxon* not being allowed to carry passengers, Mr. Putnam appeared on the ship's list as " chaplain." The abduction from Haitian territory of an American citizen by the chaplain of a British vessel might have raised all sorts of international complications ; so the Haitian general's offer was reluctantly declined. Accordingly Mr. Mitchel escaped into the back parts of the island, though a search of his premises provided some useful evidence.

A GREAT SEA MYSTERY

On Mr. Putnam's return the case came up for trial in Boston. The shippers confessed the part they had played : they had consigned goods of little or no value, grossly over-insured, and had induced Captain Parker to run his ship aground so that she became a total loss and they were able to claim from the insurance companies. One firm in particular had recovered no less a sum than $5,000 on a load of rotten fish.

At the trial it transpired that the Captain had deliberately ordered the man at the wheel to steer for the reef, and that, when the *Mary Celeste* grounded, he had told the crew to go below and help themselves to refreshments.

Strange as it may seem in the light of the evidence, Captain Parker himself escaped conviction, as the jury disagreed. He died three months later, before the new trial which had been ordered could take place.

Mr. Putnam concluded his account by commenting on the strange fate which appeared to pursue anyone who had any-

THE SEQUEL

thing to do with the business. Captain Parker's mate died three months after his Master ; one of the guilty shippers committed suicide ; all the firms concerned in the fraud failed and went out of business ; the *Saxon* was wrecked with loss of life on her next voyage ; and even the schooner *Mary E. Douglas*, in which Mr. Putnam made his first trip to Haiti, came to grief a little later. It seems as though the curse which had rested upon the *Mary Celeste* was to endure even when her timbers were rotting upon Roshell's Reef.

CPSIA information can be obtained at www.ICGtesting.com
Printed in the USA
LVOW06*0302161215

466791LV00005B/8/P